MW00512021

From Job to the Shoah

From Job to the Shoah

A Story of Dust and Ashes

Reuven Travis

WIPF & STOCK · Eugene, Oregon

FROM JOB TO THE SHOAH
A Story of Dust and Ashes

Wipf & Stock
An Imprint of Wipf and Stock Publishers
199 W. 8th Ave., Suite 3
Eugene, OR 97401

www.wipfandstock.com

ISBN 13: 978-1-62564-412-1

Manufactured in the U.S.A.

In memory of my father

Larry Travis

(Leib Baruch ben Ze'ev)

"Man raises himself toward God by the questions he asks Him," he was fond of repeating. "That is the true dialogue. Man questions God and God answers. But we don't understand His answers. We can't understand them. Because they come from the depths of the soul, and they stay there until death. You will find the true answers, Eliezer, only within yourself!"

"And why do you pray, Moshe?" I asked him.

"I pray to the God within me that He will give me the strength to ask Him the right questions."

—ELIE WIESEL, *NIGHT*

Contents

Foreword

WHAT YOU ARE ABOUT to read is a unique study of the biblical book of Job. It is nothing less than a formidable post-Shoah theology. Its author strives to answer the question that would seem completely alien to the interpretation of Job:

Why did it take so long for the Jewish people to return to their land and establish their political and national sovereignty there?

The author approaches the question as a religious Jew, one who takes very seriously the words of the Torah. That Israel went into exile can be explained as the fulfillment of the Torah's warning: collective sin brings collective punishment. But because the author, as a man of deep faith and piety, believes this to be the case, he also expects the other end of the bargain to be kept. That bargain—in the form of the covenant between God and Israel—stipulates that if Israel confesses its sin, God will remember them and restore them to their land (Lev 26).

So why did it take two thousand years for God to deliver on this promise? Why couldn't the Jewish people have been allowed to return to their land and rebuild their ruins centuries ago? How do we reconcile a long, agonizing history with the clear-cut message of the Torah?

In search of an answer to this deeply unsettling question, the author did what comes naturally to many of us: he immersed himself in a work of literature. And the work he chose is one of the most profound books in the biblical canon: Job.

Job is not only a profound work; it's also enigmatic. "A sincere and upright man, God-fearing and shunning evil," Job stands out in his generation. "There is none like him on earth." He is a man of means. But then, in an instant, he loses everything—not only his wealth but also his seven sons and three daughters. What is Job's response? He arises, tears his garments, shaves his head, falls on the ground, and worships. "Naked I came from my mother's womb, and naked shall I return. The Lord gave, and the Lord has taken away. Blessed be the name of the Lord."

We are told that in all he had to go through, "Job did not sin or cast reproach upon God." What makes this statement so arresting for us as readers is that we know what Job doesn't—that God had agreed with the Adversary to conduct an experiment with Job's existence. The aim of this test was to determine if and when the faithful servant would give up believing. God and the Adversary wanted to see if Job would continue to fear God if he had to endure affliction. Thus, Job is blessing the name of God while God is playing a game with his life!

As if this were not enough, God allows the Adversary to afflict Job's body, from the sole of his foot to the crown of his head. Job then takes a potsherd to scratch himself, sitting in ashes. His wife, the one remaining member of his family, approaches him and declares: "You persist in your integrity. Just blaspheme God and die." Job refuses: "Should we accept only good from God and not accept evil?" In all of this, Job "did not sin with his lips."

This story of suffering experienced by a man of faith has resonated with readers through the ages. Many Christians link Job to the Suffering Servant of the book of Isaiah and then to the suffering figure of Jesus Christ. Many Jews understand the Jobian narrative as a discourse on the question of why bad things happen to good people. Members of both faiths take comfort and inspiration from the concluding chapter of the book, which is often translated in this way:

> Job said in reply to the LORD: "I know that You can do everything,
> That nothing you propose is impossible for You.
> Who is this who obscures counsel without knowledge?
> Indeed, I spoke without understanding
> Of things beyond me, which I did not know.
> Hear now, and I will speak;
> I will ask, and You will inform me.
> I had heard You with my ears,
> But now I see You with my eyes;
> Therefore, I recant and relent,
> Being but dust and ashes." (Job 42:1–6) (NJPS Translation)

Readers have seen in these verses a man of deep faith and humility who accepts that there are events in life beyond his comprehension. The realization of this fact—his willingness to resign himself to it or come to terms with it—offers him solace, just as it should comfort us as readers. In this same passage, God blesses Job with more wealth and children than he had at the beginning of the book. Why? Because, we are told, Job acquiesces to the inscrutable, omnipotent will of God.

In the story of how Rabbi Reuven Travis wrestled with the meaning of these lines, you will see why this interpretation, which is shared by so many Jews and Christians and which informs the portraits of Job in so many great works of art, is lamentably mistaken. The new Job that appears in Rabbi Travis's reading is not browbeaten and resigned but rather unbending and insistent. Instead of repenting, he takes comfort in his experience. And because he does not back down, he, like the patriarch Jacob wrestling at the Jabbok, wrests a blessing for his people.

This beautifully written account draws on the best Job scholarship of past and present. It is the work of another man of faith who, in Jobian fashion, does not give up in his quest for meaning. Plagued by the two thousand years of unfilled promises of the Torah, culminating in an act of genocide perpetrated against the Jewish people, Rabbi Travis wrestles defiantly with a text. And in so doing, he wrests a blessing for us all: a powerful interpretation of a profound work of literature, a way of thinking about two millennia of Jewish history, and a model of living life faithfully—which means, with heroic defiance.

Jacob L. Wright
Associate Professor of Hebrew Bible
Candler School of Theology
Emory University

Acknowledgments

THERE ARE THREE INDIVIDUALS I wish to acknowledge, for without their help and support, this book would not have come to be.

First, I want to thank my dear friend Joseph Skibell. A talented writer and teacher, he was one of the first people to whom I confided my ideas on Job and my seemingly crazy fantasy of putting my thesis to paper. Joseph insisted that I do it. And so I did. Joseph read my early drafts and convinced me that there was something there worth reworking and revisiting. His suggestions, especially for to how my make my own voice more prominent in the book, were especially valuable.

Next is another close friend and gifted scholar of theology, Jacob Wright. When Jacob heard I was trying to write a book about Job, he insisted on reading my manuscript, and when he finished it, he insisted that it could and must be published. His unwavering belief that I had something new and important to say about Job kept me focused through every edit and reworking of this book.

Finally, I offer my most sincere thanks to my daughter Rachel. Throughout her college years, Rachel would ask me to read and edit virtually every paper she wrote, something I was delighted to do, as we share a passion for Jewish law, history, and ritual. Over the years, we spent countless hours on the phone discussing her classes and her writings, which inevitably led to bigger discussions, be they about life and religion or about dreams and aspirations. And when I told Rachel that I was planning to write a book, she saw, I think, a way to repay me for the hours of reading and proofing I had done, which is why she quickly offered to return the favor. I accepted without hesitation. And truth be told, the best part of the process of crafting this book has been the interactions I have had with Rachel. If no other person had read my manuscript, it still would have been one of the most worthwhile endeavors of my life because of the time and discussions and debates she and I shared as a result of it.

CHAPTER 1

The Question Posed

THIS IS NOT A scholarly work, notwithstanding the significant research that undergirds it or the hundreds of footnotes that support its thesis and conclusions. Nor is this a reflective journal, although it does wrestle with life issues that have plagued me for years. Rather, it is an essay that tries to come to grips with certain core questions of mine that have become more pressing with the passage of time.

Yet, when it comes to questions, it is fair to ask this: Who am I to write a book, one that, as you will soon see, endeavors to tackle theological questions and academic quandaries deemed unanswerable by many? After all, I am, in the words of my teachers' teacher, merely a *melamed*, the Hebrew term for a teacher. I do have Orthodox ordination, and I hold master's degrees in Judaic Studies and in education, but these I pursued for the sole purpose of making myself a better teacher, not a scholar.

So why write this book?

The answer to this question will unfold in the pages and chapters to come. However, in simplest terms, I write because of a theological question that has burned in my core for more years than I can count: Why is it that after thousands of years of unrequited hope and disappointment, it was only in the twentieth century that the Jewish people were able to return to the land of Israel, their historic homeland, and reestablish their political and national sovereignty there?

Long have I pondered and studied this question. And on the two occasions when I lived and worked on a kibbutz in Israel, it troubled and perplexed me to no end, in no small measure due to my belief in God. For

1

me, the fall of Jerusalem and the exile of the Jewish people, not once but twice, and the restoration of their sovereignty over their historic homeland in 1948, were not the logical consequences of a series of political machinations. Nor did they simply "just happen." I may not understand why and how these events occurred, but I have no doubt that God's hand was behind each of them.

Another crucial element that gives force to my question is the promise God made to Abraham, the first Jew, that the land of Israel would ultimately belong to him and his descendants. God repeats this promise to Abraham's descendants, Isaac and Jacob, explaining to all three that Abraham will not possess the land during his lifetime.[1] Indeed, a period of four hundred years will pass from the birth of Isaac until Joshua leads the people triumphantly into the land after their forty years of wandering through the wilderness.[2] The Jewish people did not doubt God's promise, not during this four-hundred-year period nor during the nearly 1,900 years between their exile at the hands of the Romans and United Nations General Assembly Declaration 181, passed in November 1947, which authorized the establishment of a Jewish state in what was then called Palestine.[3] How could they, given God's unequivocal promise to Abraham?

> And I will establish My covenant between Me and between you and between your seed after you throughout their generations as an everlasting covenant, to be to you for a God and to your seed after you. And I will give you and your seed after you the land of your sojournings, the entire land of Canaan for an everlasting possession, and I will be to them for a God.[4]

1. See Gen 12:7; 13:14–15; 15:7, 13 for the promise to Abraham. God repeats this promise to Isaac in Gen 26:2–4 and to Jacob in Gen 28:13. Unless noted otherwise, all English translations of biblical passages and of Rashi's commentary on the Bible come from the *Judaica Press Complete Tanach*, available online at http://www.chabad.org/library/bible_cdo/aid/16403.

2. See Rashi on Gen 15:13.

3. I do not mean to suggest that there were never individuals—or even sizable groups of individuals—who did doubt. Consider, as just one example, the Jews of the Reform movement in Germany who, during the 1800s, spoke of Berlin as their "New Jerusalem." Similarly, I not wish to belittle the heartfelt rationales for their doubts. Rather, I am here addressing the Jewish nation's collective longing for a return to its homeland, a longing that became over the centuries a central motif of many traditional Jewish prayers and rituals. It is in this context that I speak of "the Jewish people" and their desires, dreams, and aspirations, and I will use this rhetorical device throughout this book.

4. Gen 17:7–8.

While trusting in His words, the Jewish people did try God's patience. Sometimes it was by ignoring His laws. Sometimes it was with their inappropriate speech or their improper conduct in business.[5] And sometimes it involved the three cardinal sins of idolatry, murder, and sexual promiscuity. God tells them in advance what will occur should they sin, devoting two entire chapters in the Torah to this.[6] Despite God's harsh warnings, the Jewish people did sin, and, as biblical scholars and theologians tell us, the consequences foretold by God did come to pass. The Jews were exiled from their land; yet they did not lose hope that their repentance would ultimately be accepted by God and that they would ultimately return to their land.[7] Had not God told them that "despite all this, while they are in the land of their enemies, I will not despise them nor will I reject them to annihilate them, thereby breaking My covenant that is with them, for I am the Lord their God. I will remember for them the covenant [made with] the ancestors, whom I took out from the land of Egypt before the eyes of the nations, to be a God to them. I am the Lord"?[8]

This promise by God fueled centuries of both longing and disappointment on the part of the Jews and gave birth to countless of their penitential prayers and fast days intended to prove the sincerity of their repentance. And still the promise went unfulfilled, at least until our lifetime, leaving me to ask, why is it that now, after nearly two thousand years of exile, the Jewish people merited return to the land of Israel?

Coming to grips with this question would take years of thought and musing, and like many of life's great explorations, mine began in the most thrilling and mundane of places, a classroom, After returning to the States

---

5. "Their tongue is a deadly arrow, it speaks deceit; each one speaks peaceably with his mouth to his neighbor, but in his heart he lays a trap for him. Shall I not punish them for these things, says the Lord, shall I not avenge Myself on a nation such as this?" (Jer 9:7–8).

6. See Lev 26 and Deut 28.

7. This is an unwavering tenet of Jewish law, as *Aruch Hashulchan* says: "We do not recite *Tachnun* [the penitential prayer recited daily except for the Sabbath, holidays and a few other special occasions] or *Selichot* on Tisha B'Av [the day on which the Jewish people mourn the destruction of both the First and Second Temples] because it is called a *Moed*, nor do we fall on our arms [*nefilat apayim*]. For this reason, we do not recite *Tachnun* on the *mincha* prior to Tisha B'Av. This is symbolic of our confidence that HaShem will convert Tisha B'Av into a holiday" (*Aruch Hashulchan* 552:14). [author's translation]

8. Lev 26:44–45. God reiterates this promise in Deuteronomy, where He states, "For the Lord your God is a merciful God; He will not let you loose or destroy you; neither will He forget the covenant of your fathers, which He swore to them" (Deut 4:31).

from a kibbutz sojourn with my family, I began a professional transition into teaching, a process that included earning a master's degree in Judaic Studies. One course in particular had a profound impact on me. It was a seminar on *teshuvah* (repentance), and I remember a day when we had a guest lecturer, a Lutheran minister of German descent who taught theology at one of the local colleges in Chicago.[9] He did not lecture on repentance, although he did share with us tales of his father's opposition to the Nazis (which landed him in jail and eventually led to his fleeing Germany with his family). I think, but I am not sure, that he spoke about theological issues in general. The one part of his lecture that I remember very, very well (and that I kept the notes on for years afterwards) dealt with a seemingly minor point about the book of Job. I label it minor because he talked of linguistics and grammar, not theology or philosophy. He spoke about Job's final concession to God, focusing specifically on a phrase translated from the Hebrew in a number of different sources as "Wherefore I abhor myself, and repent in dust and ashes [*afar va-eifer*]."[10] He was bothered greatly by this verse. He said that he thought this translation was forced, that whereas most translations had Job referring to himself with the words *afar va-eifer*, he thought the Hebrew was not so clear. He maintained that the phrase *afar va-eifer* could just as easily be translated as referring to God. In his reading of the text, Job was calling God "dust and ashes," with the verse having the

---

9. Walter L. Michel was a professor of Old Testament at the Lutheran School of Theology in Chicago from 1972 to 2001. In an unpublished paper on the book of Job, he wrote, "I have never been satisfied with any one of the ancient or modern translations, including my own, until the spring of 1994. Finally (after more than 30 years of study with intense emphasis on Northwest Semitic studies as practiced by M. Dahood), the book of Job seems to make sense to me. Paying close attention (1) to the consonantal text (which invites the reader to try various readings); (2) to our better understanding of Hebrew *lexicography*; and (3) to the re-discovery of many *poetic devices* (mainly because of the discovery of the Ugaritic texts in 1929), I propose a different reading and understanding of *Job* 42:5–6, which, in turn, points to a different understanding of the God-Speeches and of the Epilogue" (Michel, "Did Job Or God Repent?"). It was this different understanding that he discussed during our lecture.

10. Job 42:6. This translation comes from the King James Version and is consistent with those of the American Standard Version, the New Advent Bible, the Douay Rheims Bible, the Revised Standard Version, and the New International Version. The Jewish Publication Society (JPS) translation dating to 1917 has Job speaking even more self-critically: "Wherefore I abhor my words, and repent, seeing I am dust and ashes." The 1985 revision to the JPS translation softened its wording considerably: "Therefore I despise [my life], and I will be consoled on dust and ashes." However, in a subsequent revision dating to 1999 the JPS translation reverted to the more traditional reading: "Therefore, I recant and relent, Being but dust and ashes."

sense of something akin to "I will be quiet, seeing that You are dust and ashes."

Now, this caught my attention. Job referring to God, not himself, as dust and ashes? What was Job thinking? Did he somehow believe he could curry God's good graces with this turn of a phrase? Did he really expect God to respond favorably to this verbal sparring? More importantly, how dare he, this man described in the open of the book of Job as "sincere and upright, God-fearing and shunning evil,"[11] refer to God in such a manner? And if he truly did so, what did this mean for my religious *Weltanschauung*? If this guest lecturer's linguistic analysis was correct, how was I to understand not only the ending of the book, but the entire story of Job?

Unlike my musings upon the theological underpinnings for the restoration of Jewish sovereignty over the land of Israel, these questions about the book of Job were intellectually and textually based. In other words, they could be researched and either supported or rejected.

More important, in my post-Israel period, these questions were just the distraction I needed.

One of the first sources I considered in examining the book of Job was written by William Safire. Yes, that William Safire, the longtime columnist for the *New York Times*. I used to read his op-ed pieces religiously (in both senses of the word). In 1992, Safire released a book he titled *The First Dissident: The Book of Job in Today's Politics*. I purchased it as soon as I could. William Safire, politics, and a biblical theme in one package. I could not have asked for more in a book. I found it most enjoyable and thoroughly interesting, and once done, I was eager for additional and more-scholarly analyses.

Next came Robert Eisen's *The Book of Job in Medieval Jewish Philosophy*. A classic in the field, it discusses many of the most important Jewish commentaries on Job. Eisen's book is a wonderful resource, and it was particularly helpful because it forced me to consider what I was setting out to do, for by this point I was so intrigued with the questions surrounding Job's use of *dust and ashes* that I was determined not only to work out a palatable answer in my own mind but also to put it down on paper.

Unlike Eisen's layered and complex work, the essay I had in mind when I started thinking about writing what would become this book was much more straightforward. I wished to determine, at least to my own satisfaction, who or what really is *afar va-eifer*. Said differently, I wanted to know

11. Job 1:1.

5

what the Jewish *meforshim* (commentators) and the scholarly literature had to say on the subject and to see if their insights jived with the thoughts I had had since reading William Safire and listening to that Lutheran minister those many years ago.

When I started my research on the book of Job, I was uncertain if my attempts to explain its ending were new or were even supported by the text itself and by scholars thereof. By the time I actually began writing this work, I was sure that my arguments were both new and borne out by a careful reading of the text. More important, and rather unexpectedly, resolving the question of who really is dust and ashes gave me a new understanding of my formerly unanswerable questions about the modern state of Israel.

Let me explain.

I believe that the key to understanding the book of Job is understanding Job's final remarks to God. Whatever Job's intent, his remarks, which included the phrase *dust and ashes*, found favor with God. God restores Job and then chastises Job's so-called friends. What I hope to establish in the following chapters is that it took the Jewish people until 1948 to come to grips with the theological implications of *dust and ashes* as it relates to their relationship with God. Specifically, I am convinced that it was only when the Jewish people confronted God with the same intent as did Job that God restored their sovereignty over the land of Israel.

It all seems so straightforward when laid out in a few simple sentences. But arriving at a full understanding of Job's use of the phrase *dust and ashes* is a complicated affair. Using it in turn to explain the theological underpinnings of nearly two thousand years of exile suffered by the Jewish people is more complex still. Admittedly, my attempts at explaining both *dust and ashes* and the end of the long Jewish exile are not the only possibilities. Nonetheless, I believe that my proposed reading of *dust and ashes* is not only reasonable but is also supported by the text of the Jobian narrative and by the traditional Jewish views of the people's historical suffering.[12]

---

12. "For while defeat indeed brought down Israel's first states (the Kingdom of Israel in 722 B.C.E., and of Judah in 587 B.C.E.), it simultaneously gave birth to a national consciousness among their former inhabitants. To be sure, this collective identity owed its formation to a number of preexisting factors, such as a confined and remote core territory, a history of tribal allegiances, a common language and culture, a set of shared laws and rituals, and ongoing military conflicts that fostered solidarity among allies. But by far the most important factor, we shall see, was the biblical authors' anticipation of the kingdoms' downfall. Why should this be so? The answer is as obvious as it is overlooked: A nation needs a narrative" (Wright, "A Nation Conceived in Defeat," 85–86).

CHAPTER 2

Job Revisited

BEFORE US WE NOW have two difficult and seemingly unrelated questions, one involving the restoration of Jewish sovereignty over the land of Israel and the other involving Job's use of the phrase *dust and ashes*. A careful and critical review of the book of Job (including its basic narrative and enduring themes) is necessary to answer the latter but will also, as we shall see, shed light on the former.

"There was a man in the land of Utz, whose name was Job; and that man was blameless and upright, one who feared God, and turned away from evil" (Job 1:1). Thus begins the book of Job. Our protagonist is portrayed as an extremely pious man. Prosperous, blessed with seven sons and three daughters, he is described as "the greatest of all the people of the East" (1:3). Yet he worries constantly about his children, fearful that his sons have sinned by "cursing God in their hearts" (1:5). And so he habitually offers burnt offerings as a pardon for their possible transgressions.

Job's trials and tribulations are set in motion with the appearance of "the sons of God [*benei elohim*]" (1:6).[1] This gathering of individuals, be

1. The phrase *benei elohim* is understood by most commentators to refer to angels, a view consistent with the traditional notion of a heavenly court that presents itself daily before God. There is one notable exception to this interpretation of *benei elohim*: Saadiah ben Yosef Gaon (b. Egypt 882/892, d. Baghdad 942) suggests that they are not angels but human beings who live in the land of Utz along with Job. *Benei elohim* are depicted by Saadiah as "God's beloved" in accordance with the translation of the term *ben* as "beloved," even though it is usually understood as "child." (See Eisen, *Book of Job*, especially chapter 2, in which he reviews and analyzes Saadiah's commentary on Job.) According to Saadiah, these people are beloved by God because they gather at regular intervals

they angels or men, is led by Ha-Satan,[2] and God's interaction with Ha-Satan begins simply enough. He asks Ha-Satan where he has been, and Ha-Satan answers dutifully, giving an account of his absence from the celestial court. God then asks him his opinion of Job. By selecting for consideration a man so morally pure and worshipful as to be unlike any other on earth, God seems to be taunting the member of his heavenly court whose assignment it is to be skeptical of man's goodness.[3] The Accuser rises to the challenge. "Does Job fear God for nothing? Haven't You made a hedge around him, his household, and all that he has on all sides? You have blessed the work of his hands, and his livestock has spread out in the land" (1:9–10). Here, the Accuser implies that Job's piety is solely due to his great wealth and the respect it has garnered him among his peers. And then he takes the next step. He suggests that God test the validity of his accusation: "stretch

---

to worship him. Indeed, they are described on two separate occasions in the first two chapters as coming "before the Lord."

2. The majority of English translations unfortunately render this word as *Satan*, a designation that misleadingly associates this character with the Devil or Satan of later Christian theology. The single Hebrew word *Ha-Satan* is actually made up of two elements (*ha* + *satan*). The word *satan* is a common noun meaning "adversary" or "accuser." It is used in the Hebrew Bible to describe both human (1 Sam 29:4; 2 Sam 19:22) and superhuman beings (1 Kgs 11:14, 23, 25). With its use of the definite article (*ha*), the Hebrew word *Ha-Satan* is more correctly translated as "the Accuser" or "the Adversary." The terms *the Accuser* and *Ha-Satan* will be used interchangeably throughout the remainder of this book.

Rabbi Moshe ben Maimon, also known as Maimonides or the Rambam, was one of the greatest Torah scholars of the Middle Ages and a preeminent medieval Jewish philosopher. Maimonides has a distinct understanding of the Satan and his role in the book. He maintains that all intelligent people, even those who believe that Job was a historical individual, agree that Satan is an allegorical figure. However, for Maimonides, Satan is no ordinary allegorical figure. As he opines in *The Guide for the Perplexed*, Satan is one "to which extraordinary notions and things that are the mystery of the universe are attached" and through an understanding of the book of Job's portrayal of Satan "great enigmas are solved, and truths than which none is higher become clear" (Maimonides, *Guide for the Perplexed*, 486).

The common reading of the text portrays Ha-Satan as an angel (and not as someone coequal to God). This latter point cannot be overly stressed, for in all periods of Jewish thought—from biblical to rabbinic—Ha-Satan is always subservient to God and never His coequal (see Gordis, *Book of Job*, 14). This stands in stark contrast to mainstream Christianity, in which Satan is called "the ruler of the demons" (Matt 12:24), "the prince of the world," (John 12:31) and even "the god of this world" (2 Cor 4:4).

3. Safire, *First Dissident*, 4. Safire does a particularly excellent job of summarizing and commenting on the story in the first chapter of his book.

forth Your hand and touch all that he has." Then, suggests Ha-Satan, Job will certainly "blaspheme You to Your face" (1:11).

God immediately takes up the challenge.[4] "Now the Lord said to the Adversary, 'Behold, all that he has is in your hands; only upon him do not stretch forth your hand'" (1:12). God gives Ha-Satan permission to destroy Job's possessions and family, which Ha-Satan of course proceeds to do. All of Job's possessions are destroyed. His vast herds of sheep, asses, and camels are stolen or slaughtered. His home is destroyed by a great wind. All of his offspring are killed. Yet, Job does not curse God. Instead, he shaves his head and tears his clothes, exclaiming, "From my mother's womb, I emerged naked, and I will return there naked. The Lord gave and the Lord took; may the name of the Lord be blessed" (1:21). Job, the pious man, the greatest of the people in the East, responds to his suffering as he had responded to the possible sinful activities of his children. He worships God.

At this point, the Accuser seeks and receives permission from God to up the ante. He is now free to afflict Job's person, stopping short only of taking the man's life. Ha-Satan therefore strikes Job with dreadful boils, leaving him seated in ashes and scraping his skin with broken pottery. Although Job's wife is spared physical trauma, she suffers nonetheless. Her pain over the loss of her ten children must be as great as Job's, and she must additionally care for her outcast and afflicted husband. The strain on her is apparent as she agonizingly advises Job to "blaspheme God and die" (2:9). And Job's response to all this? "You talk as one of the disgraceful women talks. Shall we also accept the good from God, and not accept the evil?" (2:10). In the end, Job rejects his wife's counsel. He reminds her that one who accepts God's blessings must be prepared to accept His burdens. As the story relates, he did not sin with his lips.[5]

Though it may seem at this point that he is losing his bet, Ha-Satan is not prepared to concede. Perhaps there are others who may yet persuade Job to turn against God and thus prove the Accuser correct. "Now when Job's three friends heard of all this evil that had come upon him, they came each from his own place, Eliphaz the Temanite, Bildad the Shuhite and Zophar the Na'amathite. They made an appointment together to come to condole with him and comfort him" (2:11). These eminent Eastern chieftains

4. Why He does so is an excellent question but is beyond the scope of this study.

5. Talmudic scholars, as well as modern exegetes, understand these words—that Job did not sin with his lips—to suggest that the apparently patient Job might have begun to formulate sinful thoughts about God's justice in his heart. Is this reading too much into the text? Perhaps, but this is a point to be considered in our next chapter.

come from afar to console their friend Job. They sit on the ground with him for a week, in silence, because they see that he is suffering and in great pain. But their sympathetic presence brings no comfort to Job, who "opened his mouth and cursed the day of his birth" (3:1).

This anguished cry of Job seems to go beyond lamentation to outright blasphemy. In cursing the day of his creation, Job is implicitly cursing his Creator—the One who brought the order and the light of day to the chaos of night. As Safire notes, "damning God's day damns God. To drive that shocking point home, Job also mocks God's first words in *Genesis*, 'Let there be light,' when he says of his own birthday, 'May that day turn to darkness.'"[6]

Job's friends are shocked and stunned. The senior member of the trio, Eliphaz the Temanite, tries to comfort Job. "Behold, you have instructed many, and you have strengthened the weak hands. Your words have upheld him who was stumbling, and you have made firm the feeble knees" (4:3–4). Yet Eliphaz politely and rhetorically suggests that an innocent man cannot be punished without good cause. "Think now, who that was innocent ever perished? Or where were the upright cut off? As I have seen, those who plow iniquity and sow trouble reap the same" (4:7–8).

This is just the start. Job's friends do not waver in their belief that he must have sinned. Only God is pure, and thus, human beings must accept some punishment for their inescapable impurity. In their worldview, God always rewards good and always punishes evil. There are no exceptions. There seems to be no room in their understanding of God for divine discretion and mystery in allowing and arranging suffering for purposes other than retribution. This explains why, as their speeches progress, they increasingly berate Job for refusing to confess his sins, even though they themselves are at a loss as to which sin he has committed.

Job, however, is unrepentant, both figuratively and literally. "Teach me, and I will be silent; make me understand how I have erred" (6:24). He is confident of his own innocence and maintains that his suffering is unjustified. In fact, he seems to accuse God of punishing him without good reason. "I would even exult in pain unsparing; for I have not denied the words of the Holy One" (6:10).[7] And though he does not curse God's name, Job does turn on Eliphaz, whom he sees as disloyal. "He who withholds kindness from a friend forsakes the fear of the Almighty. My brethren are

---

6. Safire, *First Dissident*, 7.

7. Though God does have a reason, namely, His contest with Ha-Satan, Job is painfully unaware of this.

treacherous as a torrent-bed, as freshets that pass away, which are dark with ice, and where the snow hides itself. In time of heat they disappear; when it is hot, they vanish from their place" (6:14–17).

Such a demand for loyalty in the face of what seems to be a loss of faith is extraordinary. Job is insisting that his friends remain loyal even as he begins (at least in the mind of Eliphaz) to turn away from fear of or faith in the Almighty. Job, it seems, accuses his friends of treachery for siding with God against him. "You would even cast lots over the fatherless, and bargain over your friend" (6:27).

In contrast to the gentleness and tact of Eliphaz, Bildad the Shuhite shows no pity for Job's pain and denounces his long-winded ramblings. "How long will you speak such things, seeing that the words of your mouth are [like] a mighty wind? Does God pervert judgment, or does the Almighty pervert justice?" (8:2–3). Bildad does not think so. He opines that Job's worst fear has come to pass, namely, that his sons' misconduct is the source of the suffering brought down upon Job. "If your children sinned against Him, He sent them away in the hands of their transgression" (8:4). More significant, Bildad stands firm against Job and steadfast in his conviction that God is just in His ways. "Behold God will not reject the innocent, nor will He uphold evildoers" (8:20).

Bildad's diatribe forces Job to respond, and Job does not appear ready to back down from his belief that God has perverted justice in his case. To the contrary, he is so convinced of the correctness of his complaint that he contemplates defying God's judgment by bringing Him before a court. "For if I am right, I will not reply; will I supplicate my Judge?" (9:15). Ultimately, Job concludes that this is a ridiculous notion, for it would not and could not be fair. Would God not simply overwhelm him? "If it is a trial of strength—behold He is mighty; and if of judgment—who will summon me?" (9:19). This in turn depresses Job. Power triumphing over justice? What could be more immoral than this? "The earth has been given into the hands of a wicked one" (9:24). And then another original thought pops into his mind: if only there were one who could arbitrate between them, one who could impose his authority on both God and Job. As Safire wryly notes, "with an attorney or some other interceder or intermediary between the presumptuous mortal and the easily offended God, Job might be able to speak up."[8] Job himself states, "I will speak and I will not fear Him" (9:35) if such could come to pass.

8. Safire, *First Dissident*, 9.

Now it is the third friend, Zophar the Na'amathite, who weighs in. "Should not a multitude of words be answered, or should a talkative person be accounted right?" (11:2). Unlike Eliphaz, who sees in Job's plight the inevitable outcome of a world in which all men are impure, or Bildad, who believes that Job's suffering is punishment for his children's misdeeds, Zophar rebukes Job directly. Job's punishment can only be the result of his own secret and substantial sin, a sin so horrific that Job must be hiding it even from himself. "But would that God would speak and open His lips with you, and tell you mysteries of wisdom, for the wisdom is double, and know that God lends you of your iniquity" (11:5–6). In Zophar's mind, Job is not suffering unfairly; he is not suffering enough!

Job responds to Zophar's accusation with sarcasm—"No doubt you are perfect men and absolute wisdom is yours"—and then with anger—"I am not inferior to you. Who does not know such things as these? I am a laughingstock to my friends; I, who called upon God and He answered me, a just and blameless man, am a laughingstock" (12:2–4). Job goes on to contemplate God's world and His mastery thereof in a speech that requires careful consideration by his listeners.

> He uncovers deep things out of darkness and brings to light the shadow of death. He makes nations great and destroys them; He spreads out the nations and leads them. He takes away the intelligence of the heads of the people of the land, and He causes them to wander in a wasteland [that is] not a road. (Job 12:22–24)

Job seems to be asking whether God's world is a perfect and just one. Is it not laden with violence and destruction, all of which come from Him? Some see in this speech a fundamental shift in the tone of the book, from a divine test of Job's faith to a human test of God's morality.[9] More traditional readings, for example that of Saadiah, maintain that Job's words simply reflect his belief that God's actions are beyond human reproach, even if they seem to be—and may in fact be—arbitrary.

Yet, it must be said that a simple reading of the text seems to militate against the traditional approach of Saadiah and those commentators who follow him. Job's contempt for his three so-called friends is now obvious, and he bristles at what he perceives to be the injustice of his suffering.

> But you combine lies; all of you are quacks. Would that you kept silent, and it would be accounted as wisdom for you. Hearken now

---

9. Ibid., 10.

to my reasoning, and listen to the contentions of my lips. Will you speak unjustly for God, and will you speak deceitfully for Him? Will you show Him favor? Will you contend for God? Will it be good when He searches you out? Will you mock Him as one mocks a mortal? (Job 13:4–9)

How one understands the key line of this discourse—"Behold, let Him kill me, I will hope for Him; but I will prove my ways to His face" (13:15)—ultimately lies in how one understands the outcome of the book. Are these words of faith and submission? Courage and defiance? I believe that we can only ascertain Job's true intent here after we determine how to answer what I see as the central question underlying his interactions with God, namely, who really is *afar va-eifer,* that is, dust and ashes?

In the two cycles of argument that ensue, Eliphaz—now thoroughly incensed by Job's personal baiting and evident impiety—clings to the idea that God treats men as they justly deserve. He claims that Job is being punished for good and moral cause. "Shall a wise man raise his voice with opinions of wind, and does he fill his belly with the east wind? To debate over a matter from which he derives no benefit and words in which there is no avail? Surely you will do away with fear and increase speech before God. For your iniquity teaches your mouth, but you should have chosen the tongue of the crafty. Let your own mouth condemn you and not I, and let your own lips testify against you" (15:2–6). To Eliphaz, it is clear that Job's stiff-necked and irreligious attitude prove him to be wicked. There is no injustice here, the three visitors claim. If Job had not done wrong, he would not be a victim.

In response, Job insistently swears that he has trod the ethical path, and by this he does not simply mean he has avoided seriously sinful acts. He specifies under oath how he has lived up to the moral requirements of everyday life. Consider these protestations as an example:

Will He not see my ways and count all my steps? Whether I went with falsehood, and my foot hastened upon deceit. May He weigh me with a just scale and may God know my innocence! If my foot has turned away from the road and my heart has gone after my eyes and any wrong has clung to my hands, may I sow and another eat, and produce be uprooted. If my heart was enticed to a woman, and if I lurked at my neighbor's doorway, may my wife grind for someone else, and may others kneel over her. For that is lewdness, and it is iniquity deserving punishment. (Job 31:4–11)

Here Job is obviously and openly challenging God. Job seems to say that were he lying, that is, had he in fact committed any of the sins he vociferously denies committing, God would be obligated to dole out the punishments specified for such acts. Conversely, it seems, Job is arguing that if he has in fact lived a blameless and upright life, then God has seemingly acted in an unjust manner. Job essentially gives God three choices: to punish him, to answer him by ending the inexplicable sufferings he has been enduring, or to provide him with an explanation as to why the innocent suffer.

By the end of chapter 31, Job has attempted to shift the burden of proof to God. He himself is spent, conceding that his "words are ended" (31:40). But they are not, especially with the entrance of Elihu in chapter 32.[10]

Some scholars posit that Elihu's speeches are guided and formed by his desire to serve as an "arbiter" (Hebrew, *mochiah*) between Job and God.[11] According to this view, Elihu believes that the dialogue between Job

---

10. A focal point in studies of the book of Job has been the contribution of Elihu and his speeches to the arguments advanced both by Job and by his three so-called friends. Significantly, Elihu is the only character in the book with a Hebrew name, and its meaning ("My God is he") is highly significant. Moreover, Elihu's name is nearly identical with that of the prophet Elijah ("Yah is my God"), a figure regarded in rabbinic literature as the forerunner of God and the herald announcing his kingdom. In the book of Job, Elihu similarly precedes "the Lord speaking out of the whirlwind" (38:1), and his speeches serve primarily as a transition from the dialogue with the three friends (Job 3–31) to God's speeches and direct interaction with Job (Job 38–41). "Elihu's contribution ranges anywhere from [that of] a theological bigot to a theological hero" (McCabe, "Elihu's Contribution," 47; McCabe goes on to provide an insightful summary of the various points of view vis-à-vis Elihu). Some see Elihu's speeches as little more than a rehashing of the friends' theology. Others see Elihu as an adjudicator, whereby he provides a human assessment of Job's situation and God provides the divine evaluation. Still others see Elihu as providing comic relief in an otherwise dark and disturbing story. There is even a school of thought that maintains that Elihu's speeches are a later interpolation, with some in this camp arguing that these speeches improve the friends' theology and others positing that these speeches refute their teachings. Specifically, Gordis makes an interesting and novel argument against the notion that Elihu's speeches are a later interpolation. He suggests that the central portion of the manuscript of Job suffered major accidental damage early in its history. This injury, he maintains, took place after the entire book was complete but before the Greek version (and probably the Qumran *Fragmentary Targum*) came into existence, since it reproduces our present sequence and basic text. Gordis believes that these accidents of transmission (as he terms them) affected the content of Job 24–31 and extend to the Elihu speeches in Job 32–37. He thinks that this explains the presence of difficult, even cryptic passages in the Elihu speeches (Gordis, *Book of Job*, 546–53).

11. McCabe, "Elihu's Contribution," 50–51, and reiterated by Ticciati, *Job and the*

---

and the friends has been rendered futile by the lack of an arbiter, and he steps forward to remedy the situation. Elihu claims that he will not show partiality to anyone (32:21), but it seems that this is exactly what he does do, pleading for God just as the friends have done. There is, however, a key difference between the speeches of Elihu and those of the friends. Elihu is willing to participate in Job's claims against God, claims that are often formulated in legal terms.[12] Elihu will thus respond to Job in legalistic terms and will directly cite Job's words in order to refute them. This will become clear as we study Elihu's rhetoric, which can be divided into four separate speeches.

Elihu's first speech can itself be broken into two parts. In the first (32:6–22), he informs the friends that he had been patiently waiting for them to refute Job. This they failed to do and in fact had been silenced by him. "Behold I have awaited your words; I have hearkened for your reasons, until you search out the words. Yea, I attended to you, and behold, there is no one of you to convince Job, to answer words appropriate for him" (32:11–12). Elihu thus makes clear his intent to refute Job, and in this regard, he cannot be viewed as a fourth friend. Instead, he should be seen—or at the very least, he seems to see himself—as the arbiter that Job himself had requested.[13] Elihu justifies his self-appointed role as arbiter by boasting of an internal compulsion to speak and a desire to correct the friends' failure to refute Job.

> I, too, will answer my share; I, too, will express my opinion. For I am full of words; the wind of my stomach distresses me. Behold my belly is like wine that is not opened, like new wineskins, which will burst. Let me speak so that I will be relieved; let me open my lips and reply. (Job 32:17–20)

With this as his introduction, Elihu begins the second part of this speech (33:1–33) by addressing Job directly. "But listen to my words, Job, I pray you, and hearken to all my speech" (33:1). He then challenges Job to respond to his arguments. "If you can, answer me; set up before me and stand" (33:5). And what are his arguments? Elihu summarizes Job's two main points, namely, that Job is free of sin and that being free of sin, his suffering at the hands of God is unjust. Elihu quotes Job as saying, "I am

---

Disruption of Identity, 125–31.

12. Ticciati, in chapter 5 of *Job and the Disruption of Identity*, examines the legalistic nature of Elihu's speeches in great detail.

13. McCabe, "Elihu's Contribution," 50.

innocent without transgression; I am clean, and I have no iniquity" (33:9), and a number of scholars see in these words Elihu's support for Job's claim to be without sin. Nonetheless, Elihu cannot abide by Job's assertions of injustice on the part of God. Job has often complained that God demonstrated His hostility toward him specifically by refusing to address him in a legal context. This claim of arbitrariness is a critique of God's legal authority and therefore of His commitment to justice. It is this legal accusation that Elihu seeks to answer, and for this reason, he dismisses it out of hand. "Why do you contend with Him because He does not answer any of his matters? For God answers in one way and in two, to one who does not see it" (33:13–14). God, says Elihu, does speak to man, sometimes in dreams, sometimes through a heavenly mediator when man is suffering. God's purpose in both is to turn a person from his misconduct and consequent death. "Behold God does all these, twice or thrice with man. To bring back his soul from the pit to be enlightened with the light of life" (33:29–30). Elihu closes his first speech by again challenging Job to respond. "If you have words, answer me; speak, because I wish to justify you. If not, you listen to me; be silent and I will teach you wisdom" (33:31–32).

Yet, Elihu gives Job no opportunity to respond and immediately launches into his second speech (34:1–37). Like his first speech, Elihu's argumentation in his second speech involves a summary of Job's position followed by his own refutation of this position. After inviting the wise men to listen, Elihu summarizes Job's attitude toward God's inconsistent system of justice.

> For Job said, "I am righteous, and God has deprived me of my right. Because of my sentence, I call [Him] a liar. My wound is incurable without transgression." Who is a man like Job, who drinks derision like water? [Who] went on the road to accompany workers of iniquity, and to go with men of wickedness? For he said, "A man derives no benefit when he desires [to go] with God." (Job 34:5–9)

Elihu goes on to refute Job's position with a forceful and harsh defense of God's justice in governing the world. "Far be it for God [to commit] wickedness or for the Almighty to [commit] injustice. For He recompenses man for his deed, and according to man's way He causes him to find. Surely God does not condemn and the Almighty does not pervert justice" (34:10–13). God, says Elihu, shows no partiality to rulers or to rich men. If He so wills it, He can destroy them in a moment. Or He may choose to delay their punishment, and in doing so, He certainly has good reason. Perhaps such men are meant to be instruments of His justice. Perhaps He is hoping for and waiting for their genuine repentance. In the end, Elihu appeals to Job to repent, to submit to God and ask for His guidance. In essence, Job has demanded that God present an indictment against him. This Elihu emphatically endorses. He wants Job to be tested because he believes Job is guilty of many sins, including his agreement with evildoers, his heaping up of iniquity, and his rebellion against God.

> Job does not speak with knowledge, and his words are without sense. My Father! May Job be tried to eternity, so that there be repentances among men of iniquity. For he adds transgression to his sin; among us he speaks loquaciously and multiplies his words to God. (Job 34:35–37).

Like his first two speeches, Elihu's third speech (35:1–16) involves a citation of Job's position followed by a refutation of it. In this speech, Elihu completes his principal rejoinder to Job. Job has argued that it does man no good to live in harmony with God's will. Elihu now insists on the converse, namely, that God is so far exalted beyond man that it is ludicrous to imagine that man's actions affect Him either for good or for evil. "Gaze at the heavens and see, and view the skies, which are higher than you. If you sinned, what do you do to Him, and if your transgressions are many, what do you do to Him? If you are righteous, what do you give Him? Or what does He take from your hand?" (35:5–7). As for God's silence in the face of Job's repeated protestations, this is no reflection of injustice or of God's ill will. Instead, argues Elihu, sufferers cry out merely because of the pain and not from a real desire for God's presence. God does not respond to those who pray with wrong motives or, for that matter, to those who merely cry out because of their pride and their sense of superiority to the rest of creation.

This third speech represents an oblique criticism of Job's motives in calling for God. For Elihu, it is not piety but pain that is the driving force behind Job's outburst.[14] In his fourth speech (Job 36–37), Elihu restates his essential ideas. God does not disregard or despise the righteous. When suffering comes upon them, it is meant to be a warning against sin. If they take this warning to heart, they will be restored to well-being. If not, they will suffer destruction, which is, after all, the inevitable consequence of sin.

---

14. Gordis, *Book of Job*, 397.

"If they understand and worship [Him], they will complete their days with goodness and their years with pleasantness. And if they do not take heed, they will pass away by the sword and perish because of lack of knowledge" (36:11–12). This, claims Elihu, is what God wishes to teach Job through the medium of his suffering. Elihu continues and admonishes Job. Learn from the lesson of affliction and do not be seduced by the evils of simply complaining against God! "Beware, do not turn to iniquity, for you chose this over poverty" (36:16).

Elihu's final speech concludes with a distinct shift from a defense of God's justice to praise of His incomprehensible greatness as demonstrated in His control of the elements of nature. The immediate context appears to reflect a developing storm, and in this regard, Elihu's rhetorical features also serve to set the scene for the theophany, that is, for the awesome appearance of God.[15] As Safire says, "the young man who assumed the role of God's spokesman because he was sure God was unaccountable and would never respond to the summons of Man, is thrust aside to make way for the thunderous voice of God."[16]

The contemporary rabbi and scholar David Wolpe once observed, "Challenges begin in the Bible, but do not end there. The Rabbis mock God's silence. The medieval poets recast the binding of Isaac to insist that God should not ask such sacrifices of Israel. Reb Levi Yitzchak of Berditchev took God to task for human suffering. Elie Wiesel tells the powerful story of the court in Auschwitz that put God on trial—and found God guilty. The Maggid of Zlotzov taught that the proper translation of Proverbs 3:12 is, 'The one who loves the Lord shall argue with Him.'"[17]

If one's love of God is to be measured by the vociferousness of one's arguments with Him, Job's love of his Maker runs deep indeed. Job has demanded repeatedly and vigorously that God appear and argue with him.[18]

15. McCabe, "Elihu's Contribution," 61–62.

16. Safire, *First Dissident*, 15.

17. Wolpe, "For Argument's Sake," 7.

18. Elie Wiesel, who knows about suffering and the desire to call God to account, speculates about Job's frame of mind at this point in the narrative and offers an illuminating insight: "With his undoubtedly uncalled-for insolence, he wanted to irritate God, to force Him to justify His actions even retroactively. Since punishment there was, let it at least have some basis, some motivation. He wanted it to be a result, a consequence rather than a gratuitous act. In other words, Job would have preferred to think of himself as guilty. His innocence troubled him, left him in the dark; his guilt might give the experience a meaning. He would gladly have sacrificed his soul for knowledge. What he demanded was neither happiness nor reparations, but an answer, an answer that would

Job sought to engage God, to debate and argue with Him. Yet an argument, no matter how heated or animated, presupposes a certain degree of give and take. God shows no interest in this, in carrying on a debate with Job. He will respond, but there will be no discussion, only monologue. God's response to Job begins in a divine voice described as coming from a "cloud" or "whirlwind." In Safire's words, "the Lord, apparently fed up with unending complaints about His misfeasance in office, and probably roused to wrath by the return receipt demanded by the plaintiff's oath of clearance, comes roaring out of a whirlwind to jolt Job with the most intimidating series of sarcastic questions ever posed."[19]

Not surprisingly, God opts not to address Job's suffering directly. He specifically does not do so in this discourse (38:1–40:2), and He continues to remain silent in the face of Job's attacks on His justice. God instead focuses on His sovereignty and His omnipotence, both of which He points out to Job were demonstrated in the creation of the heavens and earth. By ignoring Job's complaints and instead highlighting His own power, God underscores His pivotal role in the creation saga. He then goes on to describe for Job in powerful yet poetic language what the experience of being the Creator of the world is like.

> Who is this who gives dark counsel, with words, without knowledge? Now gird your loins like a man, and I will ask you and [you] tell Me. Where were you when I founded the earth? Tell if you know understanding. Who placed its measures if you know, or who extended a line over it? On what were its sockets sunk, or who laid its cornerstone? When the morning stars sing together, and all the angels of God shout? And [who] shut up the sea with doors when it broke forth and issued out of the womb? When I made the cloud its raiment and the dark cloud its wrapping? And broke for it My prescribed limit, and placed a bar and doors? And said, "Until here you may come but no further, and here [your strength] shall place your waves with pride." In [all] your days, did you command the morning? Did you tell the dawn its place? (Job 38:2–12)

---

show him unequivocally that man is not a toy, and that he is defined only in relation to himself. That was why Job turned against God: to find and confront Him. He defied Him to come closer to him. He wanted to hear His voice, even though he knows he would be condemned. He preferred a cruel and unjust God to an indifferent God" (Wiesel, *Messengers of God*, 223).

19. Safire, *First Dissident*, 15.

Does Job know the treasure houses of snow and hail, the path of the flood and the lightning? Has he ever begotten the rain, the dew, the frost, or the clouds? And these reveal only part of God's creative power. In a sense, this speech seems intended to make man—or perhaps better still, the man—look puny, ignorant, even meaningless.[20]

God continues and expresses His joy in the world of living creatures in a speech in which He emphasizes to Job that he shares the world with numerous powerful and remarkable creatures, creatures with lives and needs of their own, for which God must provide.[21] God's speech also highlights His sovereignty in creating and maintaining the world. The thrust is not merely that God has experiences Job does not, but also that God is King over the world and is not necessarily subject to questions from His creatures, including men. This basic theme—that the universe is a mystery to humans—is explicitly set forth in God's speeches.[22]

To Safire, God's raging reaction is exactly what Job had predicted when he expressed the wish for some intermediary to be a buffer between the accusing man and the insulted deity. "Here is powerless Man being beaten down by the God who is declaring His omnipotence—a fact never in dispute—and not even mentioning His justice, which is what concerns Man."[23] Here it seems that God is more determined to scare Job into submission than to offer a rational defense for His actions.

And what is Job's response? In truth, he really has none and merely admits that he is overwhelmed by God's power. "Behold I am of small account; what shall I answer You? I put my hand to my mouth. I said one [thing] and I will not answer, and two, and I will not add" (40:4–5). Significantly, Job does not admit that he has been wrong, nor does he apologize

---

20. Ibid.

21. Job 39:1–30.

22. Gordis, *Book of Job*, 467. There are, in addition, two other significant ideas implicit in God's first speech. Typical of Semitic rhetorical usage, they are not spelled out but are left to be inferred by the reader. The first is the fact that the universe was not created exclusively for human use and therefore neither it nor its Creator can be judged solely by human standards and goals. The second is even more significant: the natural world, though it is beyond human ken, reveals its beauty and order. It is thus reasonable for humans to believe that the universe also exhibits a moral order with pattern and meaning, though it, too, be beyond human power to fully comprehend. Per this view, who is Job—or any human—to reprove God and dispute with Him? "Will one who contends with the Almighty make himself master? He who argues with God, let him answer it" (Job 40:2).

23. Safire, *First Dissident*, 16.

for his fierce rhetoric. In fact, some scholars see in his response evasion rather than submission, which makes it understandable that God brushes it aside.[24] Since Job seems willing to let his denial of justice in the world stand, God has no choice but to address this issue head-on (40:6—41:26). And He clearly has no interest in being tactful in rebutting Job.

> Now gird your loins like a man; I will ask you and [you] tell Me.
> Will you even make void My judgment? Will you condemn Me in
> order that you be justified? (Job 40:7–8)

God here asks, Why, Job, why do you insist on condemning Me? In order that you might emerge righteous? God concedes that if Job could successfully destroy all evil in the world, He would willingly pay tribute to him (40:12–14). Some see in this concession an implication that there are some corners of the world in which God's sway is less than total.[25] This would mean that some forms of wickedness could escape His punishment. Yet even if true, this is no reason for impugning God's justice in general.

We seem at this point to be left with an unresolved question. Who has acted badly or even sinfully? The God who imposed suffering on the innocent, or the man who dared to say that this was unjust? If one is right, the other must be wrong. Yet God, as it were, ducks this question.[26]

The poetry of the book of Job ends here, but not its story. In the epilogue (42:1–17), God condemns Job's friends for their ignorance and lack of understanding while commending Job for speaking correctly. He commands the friends to prepare burnt offerings and reassures them that Job will pray for their forgiveness. Job is restored to health, gaining double the riches he possessed before. His wife bears him fourteen sons to replace the seven he had lost. His three dead daughters are replaced with three new

---

24. Gordis, *Book of Job*, 467.

25. Ibid.

26. In ducking the question, God introduces two massive creatures, Behemot (Job 40:15–24) and Leviathan (Job 40:25—41:26). Gordis offers two possible rationales for the introduction of these wondrous creatures. First, the human, who is only one of God's creatures, is neither the measure of all things nor the sole test of the worth of creation. Second, human suffering must be seen in its proper perspective within the framework of the cosmos. Evil will then seem less pervasive in the universe than Job's anguished cries have made it appear (Gordis, *Book of Job*, 467). Safire is more succinct in his understanding of these powerful and mythical creatures. To him, the introduction of these symbols of darkness and chaos seems intended to show that God's work to bring light and order cannot be judged by human standards (Safire, *First Dissident*, 17).

ones, and these are the most beautiful in the land.[27] Job is blessed once again and lives another 140 years after the ordeal, seeing his children to the fourth generation and dying peacefully of old age.[28]

27. As Safire notes, double the number of daughters would not necessarily have been considered a blessing in the ancient world, but Poet-Job showed "a curious modernity" by giving the three women shares of Job's inheritance, an unprecedented equal treatment (Safire, *First Dissident*, 18).

28. Job's reconciliation with God makes it easy to forget the loss of his children and the lingering effects of this trauma, which Job most certainly carried with him until his dying days. Elie Wiesel seems to take strong issue with those who would forget and even with Job himself: "He [Job] should have said to God: Very well, I forgive You, I forgive You to the extent of my sorrow, my anguish. But what about my dead children, do they forgive You? What right have I to speak on their behalf? Do I have the moral, the human right to accept an ending, a solution to this story, in which they have played roles that You imposed on them, not because of them, but because of me? By accepting Your inequities, do I not become Your accomplice? Now it is my turn to choose between You and my children, and I refuse to repudiate them. I demand that justice be done to them, if not to me, and that the trial continue. . . . Yes, that is what he should have said" (Wiesel, *Messengers of God*, 223). We are thus left to ponder the deaths of these children and their place in the Jobian narrative. We have already mentioned the possibility that Job's children were sinful, "cursing God in their hearts" (Job 1:5). This would explain why Job habitually tendered burnt offerings, as a pardon for their sins, and this is precisely the view articulated by Bildad. He tells Job that his worst fear has come to pass, namely, that his sons' misconduct is the source of the suffering brought down upon Job: "*If your children sinned against Him, He sent them away in the hands of their transgression*" (Job 8:4). We should also mention the opinion of Saadiah, who believes that there is one other type of trial that God can inflict upon the righteous and that is by way of "the soul"—namely, putting someone to death. God may take a righteous individual's life so as to reward him in the afterlife. Saadiah suggests that this trial was inflicted not upon Job but upon his children, who were killed. Thus, their deaths were not a result of their sinfulness but rather a reward for their righteousness. There is a biblical precedent for seeing the deaths of Job's children as an outcome of their righteousness, namely, the deaths of Aaron's two sons, Nadab and Abihu. According to Lev 10, the sons of Aaron, Nadab and Abihu, took a pan, placed fire within it, and put incense upon the fire. They brought before God this strange fire that they had not been commanded to bring, whereupon a fire came out from in front of God and consumed them; they died in front of God. Moses said to Aaron, "This is what God had referred to, 'I will be sanctified by those close to me, thus I will be honored by the entire people,'" and Aaron was silent (Lev 10:1–3). Most commentators see the actions of the sons of Aaron as sinful, although there is considerable disagreement as to the nature of their sin. For instance, the Zohar takes the actions some commentaries see as sinful and explains it as noble and righteous. According to the Zohar, the wine consumed by Nadab and Abihu was the wine Noah drank, which was in fact the wine Adam and Eve drank. This idea depends on the opinion that the tree of knowledge of good and evil was actually a grapevine and the sin of Adam and Eve was partaking of its forbidden wine. The *Leshem*, a modern-day Kabbalistic work written by Rav Shlomo Elyashiv, the grandfather of the famous *posek* (halakhic authority) Rav Shalom Yosef

This is a simple and factual reading of the epilogue, but this summary does not shed much light on what I believe to be the enduring lesson of the book. To arrive at that, we must examine Job's final response to God.

> Then Job answered God and said, "I knew that You can do everything and no design is restrained from You. Who is this who hides counsel without knowledge? Therefore, I told but I did not understand; they are hidden from me and I did not know. Hearken now and I will speak; I will ask You and [You] inform me. I have heard of You by the hearing of the ear, and now, my eye has seen You. Therefore I despise [my life], and I will be consoled on dust and ashes [*afar va-eifer*]." (Job 42:1–6)

According to Gordis, God's second speech taught Job to recognize both the mystery and the harmony of the world. "Job declares that his deepest wish has been granted, for his Maker has deigned to answer him. The beauty of his world constitutes an anodyne for his pain and serves as the basis for his renewed faith in the justice of God."[29] Not surprisingly, Gordis translates the final phrase of this response of Job as "Therefore I abase myself and repent in dust and ashes."

Safire is far less sanguine in his reading of Job's final speech. "In the prosaic epilogue, the browbeaten and awestruck Job caves in. . . . What made Job stop questioning and end his rebellion? That's left up in the air; the only motivation given by poet-Job for his character Job's total turnabout is the stunning impact of the personal encounter with God. The reason he submits is the power of personal revelation: 'now I see thee with my own eyes.'"[30] Safire, who relies on the NEB translation of the book of Job, understands the pivotal phrase in a manner similar to Gordis: "Therefore I melt away; I repent in dust and ashes."

Elyashiv, explains that Nadab and Abihu were great religious leaders and that they were trying to bring about forgiveness for the sin of Adam. This is the reason that they used "Adam's grapes"—they wished to rectify his sin. Rather than selfish sinners, they were, according to the *Leshem*, great spiritualists trying to mend the world, a view seemingly consistent with the words of God himself, "I will be sanctified through those near to Me, and before all the people I will be glorified" (Lev 10:3). Could this verse also apply to the children of Job? Perhaps, and if so, it could be an answer to the complaint of Elie Wiesel or even a comfort to Job.

29. Gordis, *Book of Job*, 491.

30. Safire, *First Dissident*, 17–18.

CHAPTER 3

The Text Parsed and Analyzed

AT THE OUTSET OF this inquiry into my unanswerable question—why the Jewish people have merited a return to the land of Israel in the last century after nearly two millennia of waiting—I noted that history, theology, and text would be our guides. Having carefully reviewed the Jobian narrative, we must now examine the text even more carefully. Remember that we are contemplating the possibility that Job refers to God with his use of the phrase *dust and ashes*. This in turn requires us to clarify what Job meant by *dust and ashes* if he in fact used it in reference to God. Ultimately, we are left to ponder how such a reading of *dust and ashes* impacts our understanding not just of the ending of the book but of the entire Jobian tale.

This is no small feat, as there are more commentaries, books, and scholarly articles on Job (both book and character) than any one person can read or process. And perhaps no part of the book of Job has been more critically analyzed—and less understood—than God's whirlwind speeches. As one leading Jobian expert has described it:

> Almost all commentators draw attention to the ambiguity and obliqueness of the divine speeches. Pages upon pages have poured from critics who puzzle over how and in what way the divine speeches serve as a reply to Job. Thus, even if the power of the divine voice shuts down explicit dialogue within the book, its teasing resistance to understanding serves to increase the flow of dialogue in the interpretive process.[1]

1. Newsom, *Book of Job*, 235.

How the divine speeches are to be understood depends in large part on how one construes their relation to other parts of the book. For instance, reading the book in a strongly unified fashion underscores the relation between the divine speeches and the narrative framework. Alternatively, it is possible to see the wisdom dialogue as the intellectual center of the book, and in doing so one may read the divine speeches as a refutation both of the friends and of Job. These and many other ways of relating the divine speeches to other voices are found in scholarly research and have yielded useful results.[2] Yet, no matter how one opts to interpret the whirlwind speeches, one thing is clear. As Carol Newsom notes, "When God speaks, it tends to bring conversation to an end. So at least it appears here, with Job initially choosing silence (40:4–5), and when forced to speak, replying briefly and apparently casting his own words in relation to the 'authoritative words of another' (42:2–6)."[3] What do these "authoritative words" convey to Job? More specifically, for our purposes, we need to determine what import they convey for the phrase *afar va-eifer*.

God certainly does not tell Job that repentance would lead to his pain being explained or his prosperity restored. Similarly, God does not give Job any verbal hint that he would be vindicated.[4] In fact, as we have previously noted, God remains silent precisely on the points Job most wants to have addressed, which both disarms and silences Job. Moreover, by maintaining complete silence on this singular issue that had brought Job to a confrontation with his Maker, God teaches His servant that he has erred in assuming that the universe operates according to a principle of rationality. "Once that putative principle of order collapsed before divine freedom, the need for personal vindication vanished as well, since God's anger and favor show no positive correspondence with human acts of villainy or virtue. Job's personal experience had taught him that last bit of information, but he had also clung tenaciously to an assumption of order. Faced with a stark reminder of divine freedom, Job finally gave up this comforting claim, which had hardly brought solace in his case."[5]

These divine speeches are particularly noteworthy because there is no literary precedent for a pair of speeches like those of Job and God, in which the voice of a sufferer stands in opposition to the response of his

2. Ibid., 237.

3. Ibid., 234.

4. Walters, "Reflections on Suffering," 447.

5. Crenshaw, *Old Testament Wisdom*, 14–15.

deity. In this respect, "what the author of the book of Job has composed is something of a tour de force."[6] Precedent or not, it nonetheless remains extraordinarily difficult to know what God intends with these whirlwind speeches. For this reason, I believe that the tone of the speeches themselves has as much impact on Job as does their content (if not more so). Could it be that the tone, not the content, shuts Job down, so to speak? William Safire thinks so, and I am inclined to agree with him. Let us return to his previously quoted description of the whirlwind speeches to see why:

> The Lord, apparently fed up with unending complaints about his misfeasance in office . . . comes roaring out of a whirlwind to jolt Job with the most intimidating series of sarcastic questions ever posed, beginning with: "Who is this whose ignorant words cloud my design in darkness? . . . Where were you when I laid the earth's foundations? Tell me, if you know . . . ." This is the scathing voice of a blustering God infuriated by Job's presumption. The doggedly questioning human, with his fierce courage and his inescapable oaths, has forced the divine hand; God, not Man, is now on trial and must defend his cosmic management. But God, as Job had feared, blows away the courtroom, resists the plea to explain his purpose in torturing Job. Instead, using lofty poetic images, God flexes his muscles and mocks the man's effrontery by showing the chasm between creator and created.[7]

Be it content or tone, the result is the same, at least initially. If God's intent is to scare Job into submission (which is how Safire reads this exchange), He succeeds. "Now Job answered the Lord and said, 'Behold I am of small account; what shall I answer You? I put my hand to my mouth. I said one [thing] and I will not answer, and two, and I will not add'" (40:3–5). However, Job's qualified submission is apparently not enough for God, who, in His second speech, becomes angrier. "Dare you deny that I am just or put me in the wrong that you may be right?" (40:8). The God of the Jobian narrative fully comprehends the zero-sum game that Job is playing. "If one is right, the other must be wrong. And God refuses to join man's game."[8]

In describing Job after the second of the two whirlwind speeches, Safire suggests that two words readily come to mind: *browbeaten* and *awestruck*. This seems an apt description when reading Job's final remarks, especially in light of his use of the phrase *afar va-eifer*. But the question remains:

6. Newsom, *Book of Job*, 238.

7. Safire, *First Dissident*, 15–16.

8. Ibid., 17.

What does Job mean with these words? Is he recanting unequivocally his earlier complaints and accusations against God? If so, the phrase *dust and ashes* need not be read as an expression of self-abasement but rather as an evocation of human dignity.[9] Alternatively, it could be that Job is being ironic in an attempt to mask his continued defiance. "By repenting sins he did not commit, by justifying a sorrow he did not deserve, he communicates to us that he did not believe in his own confessions."[10]

With such unanswered questions before us, we now turn to the text of Job's final response.

Modern scholars tend to believe that the concluding chapter of the book of Job deliberately leaves Job's reaction to God's whirlwind speeches open to interpretation.[11] For example, Newsom gives a list of five different translations of Job 42:6, and these, in her opinion, do not exhaust the various nuances and ambiguities of the Hebrew but instead suggest something of the possible range of its meaning. Newsom continues:

> Asking which possibility is correct misses the interpretive significance of the ambiguity of Job's reply, which corresponds to the ambiguity that is also part of the divine speeches. . . . The ambiguities inherent in the divine speeches and Job's reply resist every attempt to reduce them to a single, definitive interpretation. That ambiguity does not mean that a reader should refrain from arguing for a particular interpretation of the divine speeches and Job's reply, but only that a reader must recognize that more than one legitimate interpretation is possible.[12]

This is an important caveat to bear in mind as we proceed to examine how Job's concluding speech—and v. 6 in particular—have been parsed and translated over the centuries. What follows is thus detailed and technical in nature, and for this, I offer no apologies, just a warning. After all, in setting

9. Ibid., 26.

10. Elie Wiesel, from a course on the book of Job he taught on French television, as quoted in Safire, *First Dissident*, 29.

11. Thomas Krüger, a professor at the University of Zurich, provides a detailed grammatical study of the closing verses of Job's response to God in an article entitled "Did Job Repent?" He maintains that experts commonly find Job's final words to be ambiguous, and he cites a number of sources to support his argument in footnote 2 of his article. I make considerable use of Krüger's article and his research in this section of my manuscript.

12. Newsom, "Job," 629.

forth a context for my unanswerable question, I made no bones about my love for textual analysis.

According to most English versions of the book of Job, our protagonist states in his last words, עַל כֵּן אֶמְאַס וְנִחַמְתִּי עַל עָפָר וָאֵפֶר, that he "despises [or abhors] himself and repents in dust and ashes."[13] Notwithstanding this common translation, this verse is replete with semantic ambiguity, resulting mainly from the two verbs in this verse and from the overarching syntax of its two sentences.[14]

The ancient version that comes closest to the standard English translations of today is the Latin Vulgate. It reads: "Therefore I rebuke myself, and repent in dust and ashes."[15] The older Greek Septuagint, however, gives the following translation: "Therefore I held myself cheap and wasted away, and regard myself as dust and ashes."[16] "I held myself cheap" and "I wasted away" are perhaps alternative translations of the Hebrew verb סאמא. Nonetheless, it is hard to see how the clause "I regard myself as dust and ashes" is a translation of the Hebrew text as we have it today. There are a number of possible explanations for the Greek translation. Perhaps the translators had a variant Hebrew text, or perhaps they were simply unsure of the meaning of the Hebrew text and translated as best they could. It is even conceivable that they deliberately altered the original, albeit for unknown reasons.[17]

In his analysis of the variant ancient translations of Job, Krüger compares the Septuagint version to that of the Syriac Peshitta. According to Krüger, the author-translator of the Septuagint only introduces the

13. See above, n. 11.

14. Krüger, "Did Job Repent?," 218.

15. Weber, *Idcirco ipse me reprehendo.*

16. Krüger, "Did Job Repent?," 220.

17. Ibid. See also Cox, "Iob," 1–2. The difference between the Greek Septuagint and our extant Hebrew text consists not only in the translation of the second verb but also in the rendering of the tenses of both verbs in Job 42:6. The tense of the Hebrew verbs denotes the present. In the Greek version, the tense of the first two verbs, the aorist, refers to the past, here probably to the close past of the encounter with God and its immediate consequences for Job: "I held myself cheap and wasted away." The perfect tense of the third verb, then, seems to point to the present and enduring results of this encounter: "I regard myself as dust and ashes." Yet, as is well-known, the Septuagint version gives additional information about Job at the end of the book, beginning with the statement that "it is written that he will rise again with those the Lord raises up" (Job 42:17), whereas our version of the book typically reads as follows: "Then Job died, being old and sated with days." Job's self-evaluation as "dust and ashes" is thus put into perspective by the author(s) of the Greek translation (or their original, if it included this passage. See Krüger, "Did Job Repent?," 221.

notion of an eschatological consolation for Job at the end of the narrative, whereas in the Syriac Peshitta it is Job himself who speaks of his resurrection: "Therefore I will be silent and will be raised above dust and ashes."[18] Krüger further notes that the Syriac version renders the second Hebrew verb, יתמחנו, with a Syriac verb of the same root. However, in Syriac, this root no longer connoted any kind of consolation. It instead referred to the resurrection of the dead.[19]

Like the Syriac Peshitta, the Aramaic Targumim translate the Hebrew text into another West-Semitic language. The Aramaic translation included in the *Mikraot Gedolot* renders the two Hebrew verbs in Job 42:6 as "despise" and "comfort oneself." However, in its translation, these verbs have objects, something one would not expect from the context: "Therefore I despised my wealth and comforted myself over my children who are dust and ashes."[20] The present (or future) tenses of the Hebrew verbs are here transformed into the past tense.

There is an additional and significant textual variation in the Targum. In the Hebrew text (and in all other ancient versions), Job's encounter with God has him seeing God with his own eyes. This stands in sharp contrast to his former knowledge of God by hearsay. However, some manuscripts of the Targum translate Job 42:5 as "I have heard you by the hearing of the ear, but my eye has not seen you."[21] Though this translation is not consistent with the Hebrew text, it is consistent with chapters 38–41, in which Job is described as only hearing the voice of God. Still, it is possible to argue that this translation does not depart too radically from the meaning of the original. Whereas the Hebrew text's "hearing God" and "seeing God" contrast secondhand and firsthand knowledge of Him, the Aramaic version emphasizes that Job gained his firsthand knowledge by "hearing God" and not by "seeing Him." Moreover, it does not call into question that Job achieved firsthand knowledge of God via a direct encounter with Him.

In contrast, the Aramaic *Targum of Job* (11Q10) found at Khirbet Qumran, probably a first-century-CE copy of a second-century-BCE composition, affirms that Job has seen God (42:5). Its translation of Job 42:6 seems to describe the consequences of Job's direct encounter with God according to the common conviction that whoever sees God at least faints

18. Ibid.
19. Ibid.
20. Ibid.
21. Ibid., 222.

and may even die.[22] "I have heard of you by the hearing of the ear, but now my eye has seen you; for this I will be poured out and dissolved and I will turn into dust and ashes" (11Q 2–18, 11Q 20–31).

Interestingly, the approaches of early Jewish biblical commentators sometimes reflect today's standard English translations, rendering *dust and ashes* as a description of Job's search for comfort or repentance. Saadiah, for example, reads the verse as "I had heard of Thy power by report, but now have I seen it with mine eyes. Therefore do I spurn what I once said and take my solace in dust and ashes."[23] Yet others do not. Rashi[24] holds that *dust and ashes* refers to Job's ultimate passing and not specifically to his state of consolation. "I will be comforted even if I dwell in the grave, to return to the dust and ashes from which I was taken."[25]

All the versions and translations considered to this point in some way relate *dust and ashes* to Job himself. Maimonides, in his understanding of the text, does not. In his view, Job is singled out for praise by God in the final chapter of the book only because he achieves intellectual perfection and love of God. "According to Maimonides, God tells Eliphaz that he and his two friends 'have not spoken the truth about Me as did My servant Job' (42:7), because Job has just recognized in the preceding verse that physical and material well-being—'dust and ashes'—are of no importance compared to the contemplation of God that comes with the perfection of the intellect. Thus, God's praise for Job is prompted only by the latter's recantation at the end of the story."[26] In other words, Job describes neither himself nor his emotional state with "dust and ashes." He instead uses this phrase to characterize his new understanding of the worth and importance of the

---

22. Ibid.

23. Goodman, *Book of Theodicy*, 410.

24. Born in 1040, Rabbi Shlomo ben Yitzhak, better known by the acronym Rashi, was an extremely humble man who repeatedly refused to accept a rabbinic position. He taught and wrote while earning his livelihood as a wine merchant. Rashi spent almost his entire life working on his Talmud commentary. Brief, concise, and enlightening, his comments are matchless in their clarity. He also wrote a Torah commentary that is printed in virtually every edition of the Chumash. Although it is the very model of conciseness and clarity, Rashi's commentary demonstrates his great understanding of the full range of talmudic and midrashic interpretation. It is an essential tool for students of the Bible.

25. Curtis, "On Job's Response," 501 n. 14.

26. Eisen, *Book of Job*, 67.

material world, as if to say, "Wherefore I abhor all that I used to desire and repent of my being in dust and ashes."[27]

While our discussion of the linguistics of the book of Job to this point has focused on the two nouns "dust" and "ashes," the difficulties surrounding how to correctly translate Job 42:6 are further complicated by how one understands two key verbs. Modern scholars struggle with these two verbs just as greatly as did the authors of the ancient translations we have so far discussed. For example, Gordis observes that the first verb, אמאס, is not a metaplastic form of מסס, that is, "I melt," as is the case in Ps 58:5. Rather, it should be translated as "I despise my arguments" or "I abase myself."[28] Similarly, Thomas Krüger observes that the first verb, אמאס, can be understood in the sense of "reject, refuse, despise" (root מאס) or in the sense of "dissolve, melt away" (root מאס or מסס, respectively). Taking the first meaning (which is transitive), the object of rejection lies either in "dust and ashes" (which is also the object of the following verb, יתמחנו) or in the former thoughts and statements of Job, which he has to reconsider after his encounter with God. Less probable, argues Krüger, is the assumption that the verb has a reflexive sense, so that Job himself is the object of rejection or disdain. Krüger thus maintains that there are three possibilities to translate the verb אמאס:

1. *I reject (or despise) dust and ashes*—whatever the latter should mean.

2. *I reject (or despise) my former thoughts and statements.*

3. *I dissolve (or melt away)*—in the sense of dying or perhaps giving up.

The second verb, יתמחנו (נחם Niphal), has the basic meaning of changing one's mind about someone or something in the sense of "be sorry, regret" or in the sense of "console oneself." With the preposition על, the verb נחם normally means "to regret something," "to be sorry because," or "to console oneself about." Consequently, posits Krüger, the following translations seem to be possible:

1. *I regret (or am sorry because)*—a) *dust and ashes* OR b) *my former thoughts and statements*—*in dust and ashes.*

2. *I console myself*—a) *about dust and ashes* OR b) *in dust and ashes.*

3. *I repent in dust and ashes.*

Krüger further maintains that Job 42:6 can be interpreted syntactically as a string of two complete and independent sentences. The final

27. Schreiner, *Where Shall Wisdom Be Found?*, 68.

28. Gordis, *Book of Job*, 492.

phrase, "on dust and ashes," would thus be connected only with the second verb. However, this phrase can also be understood as a complement to both verbs, whether as a localization ("I melt away and console myself in dust and ashes") or as a direct object ("I reject and regret dust and ashes"). The phrase *dust and ashes* could therefore be understood as a metaphor for human beings and their insignificance in comparison to God. In fact, this is precisely the sense of the phrase as used by Abraham when arguing with God about the fate of Sodom. "And Abraham answered and said, 'Behold now I have commenced to speak to the Lord, although I am dust and ashes'" (Gen 18:27).[29]

I have relied greatly on Krüger to better understand the linguistic issues surrounding Job's closing statement, and with good reason. Most modern translators accept the position, taken by Krüger as well, against translating the verb סאמא in a reflexive sense so that Job himself is the object of rejection or disdain. Those translations which are counter to Krüger's and use phrases such as "I despise myself" are boxed in black and appear in reversed type in the table below. However, what is most noteworthy for our purposes is that only three of these, the JPS translations of 1971 and 1999 and Stephen Mitchell's 1987 translation, have Job referring to himself as either "dust and ashes" or merely "dust."

New English Bible:	Therefore I melt away; I repent in dust and ashes.
New Revised Standard Version:	Therefore, I despise myself, and I repent in dust and ashes.
New International Version:	Therefore I despise myself and repent in dust and ashes.
New American Standard Bible:	Therefore, I retract and repent in dust and ashes.
Jewish Publication Society (1917):	Wherefore I abhor my words, and repent, seeing I am dust and ashes.
Jewish Publication Society (1999):	Therefore I recant and relent, being but dust and ashes.
Contemporary English Version:	That's why I hate myself and sit here in dust and ashes to show my sorrow.

29. Aside from Abraham's use of it, the only other appearance of the phrase "dust and ashes" in the Bible also occurs in the book of Job. We will continue to examine its meaning in Job 42:6, but it is worth noting its usage in Job 30:19. There it sums up the miserable situation of Job, one which is, in his opinion, brought about by God: "It directed me to the mud, and I was compared to dust and ashes." The sense of the phrase in this instance seems consistent with Maimonides's understanding of the phrase as used in Job 42:6.

New Living Translation:	I take back everything I said, and I sit in dust and ashes to show my repentance.
Dale Patrick (1976):	Therefore I repudiate and repent of (or forswear) dust and ashes.
Robert Gordis (1978):	Therefore I abase myself and repent in dust and ashes.
D. J. O'Conner (1983):	I melt away, and I am consoled for dust and ashes.
Stephen Mitchell (1987):	Therefore, I will be quiet, comforted that I am dust.
William Brown (1996):	I hereby reject [my life], and am comforted concerning dust and ashes.
John Mark Hicks (1999):	I am little/I melt [before you], and am comforted over [my] dust and ashes.

Source: Hicks, "Faithful Lament," 18.

Why is it that Krüger's view against translating the verb סאמא in a reflexive sense seems to be broadly accepted? I have found two possibilities, both of which strike me as plausible.

The first involves how we understand the words *despise* and *reject*. Job evidently not only withdraws his charges against God but also despises and rejects his attitude of pride. Job had previously expressed remorse over his losses, but now he seemingly changes his mind and abandons his arrogance toward God.[30] "Though Job's words are sinful, these are not words of a blasphemous rebel. We must remember that many of his words have been spoken in a context where he has been wrestling to reconcile his beliefs about God with the reality he was experiencing and witnessing, and not in a context of rebellion."[31] Said differently, "he does not repent of sins that have allegedly brought on the suffering; he repents of his arrogance in impugning God's justice, he repents of the attitude whereby he simply demands an answer; as if such were owed him. He repents of not having known God better."[32]

A second goes to the core of why the book of Job was included in the biblical canon. Traditional Jewish sources frequently deal with the issue of God's involvement with or withdrawal from the affairs of humans. One of the direst warnings God gives in the Torah is the threat that "I will surely

---

30. Patrick, "Translation of Job xli 6," 369–71.

31. McCabe, "Elihu's Contribution," 68.

32. Carson, *How Long, O Lord?*, 174; see also Walters, "Reflections on Suffering," 447.

hide My face in that day for all the evil which they have wrought."[33] According to Rabbi Abraham Besdin, this suggests a suspension of the divine covenantal dialogue with Israel and a withdrawal of God's constant surveillance over its welfare.[34] The opposite pole of God's noninvolvement is the reassuring principle of *nesiat kapayim* ("turning His face unto thee"), as clearly expressed in the priestly blessing: "May the Lord lift up His countenance upon you and give you peace."[35] Here we have the active relationship restored and God's participation in human history with Israel as His agent.[36] Besdin maintains that it is precisely this tension between withdrawal and involvement that the book of Job seeks to address.

> Why, asks Job, is he subjected to such torment, since he has lived righteously? His friends suggest that it is undoubtedly a just retribution for clandestine sins. God suddenly appears, rebukes the friends and upholds Job's righteousness. No explanation for his suffering is given; puny man is challenged by God for his presumptuousness in seeking to understand His inscrutable judgment. Can man otherwise encompass in his intellect the mysteries of cosmic creation? Job is comforted and consoled, not by an explanation but by God's reassuring closeness, that He is near once again.[37]

This second view holds that the comfort and consolation most translators see in Job's use of *afar va-eifer* are built on the simple fact that God appears to him, notwithstanding the vociferous nature of the whirlwind speeches. As Martin Buber observes, "the true answer that Job receives is God's appearance only, only that distance turns to nearness, that 'his eyes see Him,' that He knows him again. . . . Nothing has happened but that man again hears God's address."[38]

In the end, we are left with many ways to translate Job's closing remarks. Do his words express regret and if so, how and to what extent? Does he truly repent and if so, from what? Does he despise life and look forward to death? One can find support in the scholarly research for each of these.

---

33. Deut 31:18. See also Deut 31:17; 32:20.

34. Besdin, "Holocaust," 141.

35. Lev 26:44.

36. Besdin, "Holocaust," 141.

37. Ibid.

38. Buber, *At the Turning*, 61–62.

What one seems not to find, however, are scholars or translators who understand Job's use of "dust and ashes" as referring to God.[39]

39. Wilson, *Book of Job*, was the only source I found for the notion that Job is referring to God with the phrase "dust and ashes." Wilson translates Job 42:6 as follows: "And so I reject [you] and I feel sorry for all humanity." His rationale is as follows: "We achieve our rendition of this difficult verse by moving the Masoretic pause ('etnak) to סאמא from יתמחנו. One might conjecture that the Masoretes understood this verse well; however they could not publish such a rejection for the 'faithful' reader" (201). We will discuss Wilson's approach in greater detail in the next section of this work.

Chapter 4

The Need to Redefine Dust and Ashes

I BEGAN MY REFLECTIONS on the book of Job by asking, who is really *afar va-eifer*? To this point, I have discussed numerous sources, almost all of which understand Job's use of this phrase as referring to himself. And although it may be linguistically possible to translate the phrase so that Job is actually describing God, I have uncovered only one source, other than that Lutheran guest lecturer from so many years ago, who subscribes to this view.[1] Yet, despite the overwhelming scholarly support for the commonly accepted translation of this phrase, it leaves me unsettled. To me, the traditional reading of this phrase seems to strip the book of Job of any unique or groundbreaking lesson.

How so?

One outcome of the traditional reading of Job is that by calling himself dust and ashes (and thus repenting of some unnamed sin), Job affirms the three friends' supposition that suffering is necessarily the result of sin. But the link between sin and punishment has already appeared elsewhere in the biblical narrative. For our purposes, perhaps the most important and most compelling of these centers on the experiences of the Jewish people during their forty years of wandering in the wilderness. God Himself says that "they have tested Me these ten times and not listened to My voice."[2] Moreover, according to rabbinic tradition, the Jewish people were punished after each of these incidents.[3] Ten times the people rebel. Ten times they are

1. See n. 81.

2. Num 14:22.

3. *b. Arakhin* 15a. (Translations of the Talmud, as well as the expository notes that

punished. Do we really need the friends' exhortations of Job to teach us the correlation between sin and punishment?

A second possibility is that Job calls himself dust and ashes not because he sinned and is remorseful but because he is cowed into submission by God's awesomeness. Accepting Job's emphatic claims that he is innocent of sin, we may view his story simply as one of suffering experienced by the righteous. But again, do we need the book of Job to illustrate this point? Does not Jacob's life, as just one example, demonstrate how even the most righteous of men suffer greatly? Jacob struggled with Esau his whole life; he had to contend with Laban for twenty years; he suffered through Rachel's premature death and then Dinah's kidnapping and rape; he had to face the aftermath of Simeon and Levi wiping out the city of Shechem; and ultimately he mourned for his lost son Joseph for twenty-two years. So harsh was his suffering that when this great man, for whom the Jewish people are named,[4] first meets Pharaoh, the latter is stunned by his appearance and asks, "How many are the days of the years of your life?"[5] Jacob's answer is rather telling: "The days of the years of my sojournings are one hundred

---

accompany them, are from Goldwurn and Scherman, *Talmud Bavli* unless otherwise noted.) The ten tests are described as follows:

"Our fathers tested God with ten tests: Twice at the sea, twice with water, twice with the manna, twice with the quails, once with the golden calf and once in the wilderness of Paran.

"Twice at the sea—once on the way down and again on the way up. On the way down—as the verse states, 'is it because there was a shortage of graves in Egypt [that you took us to die in the desert]?' (Exod 14:11). On the way up—Rabbah bar Mari said . . . the Jewish people were rebellious at that very hour, saying: 'Just as we go up from this side, so will the Egyptians go up from the other side.'

"Twice with water—at Marah and at Refidim. At Marah—as the verse states: 'They came to Marah, but they could not drink water [because it was bitter] (Exod 15:23), and the verse states: 'The people complained to Moshe' (Exod 17:3). At Refidim—as the verse states: 'They camped in Refidim and there was no water for the people to drink' (Exod 17:1), and it is also written: 'The people quarreled with Moshe' (Exod 17:2).

"Twice because of the manna—they were told, 'do not go out [to collect it on Shabbat],' but they went out (Exod 16:25–30). They were told, 'Do not leave over [until morning],' but they left over (Exod 16:19–20).

"Twice because of the quails—the first and second quails. The first: 'When we sat by the pots of meat' (Exod 16:3). With the second quails: 'The mob [among them had strong cravings]' (Num 11:4).

"With the golden calf—as it happened (Exod 32:1–29).

"In the wilderness of Paran—[the sin of the spies] as it happened."

4. "The children of Israel." The name Jacob was given upon the conclusion of his nightlong struggle with an angel (Gen 32:29).

5. Gen 47:8.

thirty years. The days of the years of my life have been few and miserable, and they have not reached the days of the years of the lives of my forefathers in the days of their sojournings."[6]

There is yet another possible outcome of Job referring to himself as dust and ashes. Perhaps Saadiah is correct that Job's suffering is merely a test and that the book of Job sets forth a model for how one should respond to such divine tests. If so, *dust and ashes* connotes neither a sense of remorse nor an act of contrition. It would instead be an expression of humility in response to the magnitude of the tests Job overcomes. However, this reading of Job also strikes me as problematic. There is no need for an additional biblical narrative describing God testing the righteous. We already have the paradigmatic example of this: does not the text of Genesis itself, supported by mishnaic and midrashic sources, show us that Abraham is the one God chooses to test and whose responses God chooses to record in his Torah?[7]

Let me say it even more strongly. The traditional reading of Job reveals the narrative to be a tale of the sometimes incomprehensible nature of suffering. Yet, I would maintain, the Jewish people did not need a parable, even one as powerful as Job's, to teach them about suffering and their inability to comprehend it. Admittedly, the Bible conveys various moral and ethical lessons in multiple texts, and thus it should not be problematic that Job's message regarding suffering is echoed elsewhere in the Bible. However, by the time the rabbis canonized the twenty-four books of the Bible,[8] the Jewish people had suffered exile and the loss of their homeland not once but twice. Given other biblical accounts of man's suffering in general and the very real suffering of the Jewish people in particular, why include a nonprophetic parable of unknown authorship in the biblical canon if not to illustrate a new or unique religious or theological worldview? In fact, many

6. Gen 47:9.

7. It is on this notion of God's testing of Abraham that Rabbi Sholom Noach Berezovsky, who served as the Slonimer Rebbe from 1981 until his death in 2000, writes so powerfully. In his magnum opus, the seven-volume *Netivot Shalom*, he points out that the Torah only uses the language of testing with Abraham and not with the other Patriarchs. "And it came to pass after these things, that God tested Abraham, and He said to him, 'Abraham,' and he said, 'Here I am'" (Gen 22:1). Similarly, *m. Avot* 5:4 uses the language of testing only with regards to Abraham, "With ten tests our father Abraham was tested and he withstood them all—in order to make known how great was our father Abraham's love [for God]." All citations of *m. Avot* herein are from http://www.chabad.org/library/article_cdo/aid/680274/jewish/Ethics-of-the-Fathers-Pirkei-Avot.htm.

8. Evidence suggests that the process of canonization occurred between 200 BCE and 200 CE.

modern Jewish readers of Job would go so far as to ask, Do we really need Job to teach us about dust and ashes when six million of us were literally turned to dust and ashes at the hands of Hitler and his henchmen? Does Job's reference to dust and ashes truly carry more weight or resonate more strongly in their hearts and minds than that of Elie Wiesel?

> Never shall I forget that night, the first night in camp, which has turned my life into one long night, seven times cursed and seven times sealed. Never shall I forget the smoke. Never shall I forget the little faces of the children, whose bodies I saw turned into wreaths of smoke beneath a silent blue sky.
>
> Never shall I forget those flames which consumed my faith forever.
>
> Never shall I forget that nocturnal silence which deprived me, for all eternity, of the desire to live. *Never shall I forget those moments which murdered my God and my soul and turned my dreams to dust.* Never shall I forget these things, even if I am condemned to live as long as God Himself. Never.[9]

In my mind, the Jewish people have sufficient biblical stories and collective historical memory to demonstrate their inability to comprehend inexplicable suffering. So I am left to ask, what unique purpose does the book of Job serve to warrant its inclusion in the Bible?

In the end, questions such as this leave me unsatisfied with the traditional reading of Job and his decisive response to God. Did he, this man described as "sincere and upright, God-fearing and shunning evil" in the opening verse of the book, need to suffer to the degree he did in order to recognize that he was but dust and ashes as compared to God?

And what of his anger and his indignation? If it was sinful, was he not manipulated by God into sinning once God challenged the Accuser? If his anger was not sinful but was instead a justified and natural reaction to his suffering, how are we to react to his being "browbeaten" into submission by God's fiery speech from the whirlwind?

How does Job repenting in dust and ashes answer any of these questions?

I don't think it does, which is why I keep coming back to the linguistic possibility that Job in fact calls God *dust and ashes* at the end of book. Leslie Wilson, the one modern scholar who rejects traditional translations and

---

9. Wiesel, *Night*, 32. Later in his work, Wiesel says, "How I sympathized with Job! I did not deny God's existence, but I doubted His absolute justice" (42).

sees Job referring to God with the phrase *afar va-eifer,* suggests that "the Masoretes understood this verse well; however they could not publish such a rejection for the 'faithful' reader."[10]

I would explain it differently. There are many examples in the Bible in which the rabbis reject the *peshat,* that is, the simple reading of the text, based on an oral tradition. The best example (or at least one of the best-known) involves Reuben's reaction to Jacob moving his primary residence to Bilhah's tent after the death of her mistress Rachel.

> So Rachel died, and she was buried on the road to Ephrat, which is Beit-Lechem. And Yaakov erected a monument on her grave; that is the tombstone of Rachel until this day. Israel journeyed, and he pitched his tent at some distance past the Tower of Eder. And it came to pass when Israel sojourned in that land, that Reuben went and lay with Bilhah, his father's concubine, and Israel heard [of it], and so, the sons of Yaakov were twelve.[11]

The simple reading of the verse suggests that Reuben slept with Bilhah. The rabbis steadfastly reject this, and their view is articulated in *b. Shabbat* 55b. Simply put, the rabbis cannot contemplate that Reuben had sexual relations with his father's concubine. They instead maintain that Reuben "disarranged" Jacob's bed, thereby "profaning it." Why would he do such a thing? They explain that when Rachel died, Jacob took his bed, which had been regularly placed in Rachel's tent, and moved it into Bilhah's tent. Reuben came and protested his mother's humiliation. He said, "If my mother's sister was a rival to my mother, should my mother's sister's handmaid now also be a rival to my mother?" For this reason, he "disarranged" it.

You may ask, on what grounds do the rabbis base this radical reading of the text? They point out that v. 22 concludes with a phrase not at all connected to Reuben's actions, namely, "and so, the sons of Yaakov were twelve." The rabbis see an important link between the two, as summarized by Rashi in his commentary. In brief, with the birth of Benjamin, the destined number of sons was completed, and it was proper that they be counted. By juxtaposing Reuben's action with the birth of Benjamin and the subsequent counting of the twelve sons, the rabbis saw in the text another critical (albeit implied) lesson: all of Jacob's sons were equal, and all of them were righteous. In other words, Reuben had not sinned.

10. Wilson, *Book of Job,* 201.

11. Gen 35:19–22.

The rabbinic logic is evident. Had Reuben actually slept with one of his father's wives, Jacob would certainly have banished him. By stating that Jacob's sons still number twelve, the verse underscores that no punitive measure was necessary because no sinful act had taken place.

Taking the phrase *afar va-eifer* to refer to God, as Wilson and now I suggest, is no more radical a departure from the simple reading of the text than is having Reuben move his father's bed (rather than sleep with his father's wife). The question is not whether this reading is linguistically feasible or whether the Sages were aware of an alternative understanding of Job's response to God. Instead, the issue is one of textual support, that is, is there a compelling reason to support an alternative understanding of *afar va-eifer*?

I think there is, although not in the book of Job itself. I believe the textual support needed to make this linguistic possibility a reality appears in chapter 2 of the creation story set forth in Genesis.

> Now the heavens and the earth were completed and all their host. And God completed on the seventh day His work that He did, and He abstained on the seventh day from all His work that He did. And God blessed the seventh day and He hallowed it, for thereon He abstained from all His work that God created to do [*la'asot*]."[12]

The final word, *la'asot*, appears both unnecessary and irregular in this context. Creation is complete, or so it seems from the simple past tense of all other verbs in this verse. What, then, did God at this point need "to do"? Based on this textual clue, the midrash teaches that God did not finish creating the world at the end of six days.[13] He left a portion of the world unfinished. He left His creation, so to speak, incomplete and imperfect. Who then will complete creation? Mankind. Perfecting God's universe is the task for humanity in general and for the Jewish people in particular. That is the lesson of *la'asot* and why its appearance in the text is not gratuitous. The word is there to teach humans that they are called upon by God Himself to be partners in completing and perfecting creation. The Zohar expresses this

---

12. Gen 2:1–3.

13. *Gen. Rab.* 11:7, which uses the expression *tzarikh tikkun*, a term sometimes mistaken as a synonym for the generic *tikkun olam*. The former more specifically means to "complete" the act of creation (as opposed to fixing or repairing it through deeds such as helping the poor or feeding the hungry). My thanks to Rabbi Dr. Michael S. Berger for pointing out this source to me.

even more succinctly: "On the sixth day, having created man, God said to him: 'I have worked heretofore, now you shall continue.'"[14]

Additional support for this insight is found in the following passage in Isaiah.

> I am the Lord your God, Who wrinkles the sea and its waves stir; the Lord of Hosts is His name. And I placed My words into your mouth, and with the shadow of My hand I covered you, to plant the heavens and to found the earth and to say to Zion [that] you are My people.[15]

The Zohar comments on the phrase "you are my people" and states: "Do not read, 'You are My people (*amee*)' but 'You are with me (*imee*).' You are my partner, my collaborator. Just as God made heaven and the earth, you must complete heaven and the earth."[16]

Contemporary scholars such as Rabbi Joseph Ber Soloveitchik[17] offer similar insights about humanity's role in the ongoing work of creation. Soloveitchik believed that the peak of religious ethical perfection to which Judaism aspires is human as creator. According to him, when God created the world, He provided an opportunity for humans to participate in His creation. "The Creator, as it were, impaired reality in order that mortal man repair its flaws and perfect it. God gave the Book of Creation—that

---

14. Quoted in Wiesel, *Messengers of God*, 35. There is a precedent for God ceding authority in certain matters and partnering with the Jewish people. The Talmud (*b. Rosh Hashanah* 25a) discusses the fact that God has given over to the Jewish people the power to declare the new moon, thereby establishing the first day of each month and the dates for any biblical holidays that might occur in a given month. This power is theirs, conclude the Sages, even should the Jewish people mistakenly declare the new moon to be on a certain day or even should they intentionally establish the new moon on the wrong day. God has given them complete discretion in this matter. Thus, although the holidays are God's, the calendar that governs them belongs to the Jewish people.

15. Isa 51:15–16.

16. Zohar 1:5a; all citations of the Zohar are from http://www.sacred-texts.com/jud/zdm/zdm010.htm.

17. Rabbi Joseph Ber Soloveitchik (1903–1993) was a talmudist and modern Jewish philosopher. He was a descendant of the Lithuanian Jewish Soloveitchik rabbinic dynasty. As *rosh yeshiva* (yeshiva head) of Rabbi Isaac Elchanan Theological Seminary at Yeshiva University in New York City, the Rav, as he came to be known, ordained close to two thousand rabbis over the course of almost half a century. He advocated a synthesis between Torah scholarship and Western, secular scholarship, as well as positive involvement with the broader community. He served as an advisor, guide, mentor, and role model for tens of thousands of Jews, both as a talmudic scholar and as a religious leader. He is regarded as a seminal figure in Modern Orthodox Judaism.

repository of the mysteries of creation—to man, not simply for the sake of theoretical study but in order that man might continue the action of creation."[18] Or as Soloveitchik says elsewhere, "God appoints man as His plenipotentiary. His agent, His *shali'ah.* . . . Since man can refuse to collaborate with the Almighty, his cooperation is the more welcome."[19]

Seen in this light, humans are not subservient to the forces of nature, nor are the forces of nature supernatural ones that are superior to humans. Humans instead stand on the side of God in taming nature and completing creation.[20] And how exactly are we, humankind, to stand with God? According to the talmudic sages, we do so by remembering that humans were created in God's image. Thus, "just as God is kind, so should you be kind; just as God is merciful, so should you be merciful; just as God is holy, so should you be holy."[21] But standing with God demands that we be more than mere reflections of Him. We must instead, to the extent possible, be full and equal partners with God. This is, of course, an impossibility. Humans can never be God's equal. What we can and must do is exercise our power to speak up and challenge God in the face of perceived wrong or injustice. This is what an empowered partner would do, and this, I contend, is exactly what Job does. He sees God as an unfair or unreasonable partner, pushing him beyond the limits that a person should be expected to suffer, and he tells God so. He calls him *afar va-eifer.* As his partner, Job tells God He has gone too far.

In the words of Rabbi Besdin, "if man is to retain his singular status as a being 'in the image of God' and not merely an automaton, he must be allowed to rebel."[22] In the case of Job, his rebellion does not manifest itself in a lack of faith but instead in a willingness to speak uncompromisingly to God. Job "rebels" in order to assert himself as an empowered partner of God. This, I think, is what God wants from us. This is what He tells us He wants from us, and there is a beautiful story (*aggadah*) that underscores this point.[23] It takes place during a *halakhic* (legal) discussion in which the

18. Soloveitchik, *Halakhic Man*, 101.

19. Soloveitchik, *Abraham's Journey*, 38.

20. Guttmann, *Philosophy of Judaism*, 88.

21. *b. Shabbat* 113b.

22. Besdin, "Holocaust," 140.

23. *Agadata* are stories that the rabbis included in the talmudic text in order to illustrate important points regarding their worldview. These stories contain a wealth of information on a broad range of topics.

rabbis debate whether an oven that has become impure can be purified. Almost all the Sages feel it cannot, but Rabbi Eliezer, a lone voice but a great scholar, disagrees.

> On that day, Rabbi Eliezer put forward all the arguments in the world, but the Sages did not accept them. Finally, he said to them, "If the *halakha* (legal ruling) is according to me, let that carob tree prove it." He pointed to a nearby carob tree, which then moved from its place a hundred cubits, and some say, four hundred cubits. They said to him "One cannot bring a proof from the moving of a carob tree." Said Rabbi Eliezer, "If the *halakha* is according to me, may that stream of water prove it." The stream of water then turned and flowed in the opposite direction. They said to him, "One cannot bring a proof from the behavior of a stream of water." Said Rabbi Eliezer, "If the *halakha* is according to me, may the walls of the House of Study prove it." The walls of the House of Study began to bend inward. Rabbi Joshua then rose up and rebuked the walls of the House of Study, "If the students of the Wise argue with one another in *halakha*," he said, "what right have you to interfere?" In honor of Rabbi Joshua, the walls ceased to bend inward; but in honor of Rabbi Eliezer, they did not straighten up, and they remain bent to this day. Then, said Rabbi Eliezer to the Sages, "If the *halakha* is according to me, may a proof come from Heaven." Then a heavenly voice went forth and said, "What have you to do with Rabbi Eliezer? The *halakha* is according to him in every place." Then Rabbi Joshua rose up on his feet, and said, "It is not in the heavens" (Deut 30:12). What did he mean by quoting this? Said Rabbi Jeremiah, "He meant that since the Torah has been given already on Mount Sinai, we do not pay attention to a heavenly voice, for You have written in Your Torah, "Decide according to the majority" (Exod 23:2). Rabbi Nathan met the prophet Elijah. He asked him, "What was the Holy One, blessed be He, doing in that hour?" Said Elijah, "He was laughing and saying, 'My children have defeated me, my children have defeated me.'"[24]

God laughs, He rejoices when humans conducts themselves like empowered partners. I believe that this is what God was looking for from Job and why He ultimately restored everything to him. And though this may not be in accordance with traditional interpretations of the conclusion of the book of Job, I am convinced that an examination of the rabbinic view of history, especially of those catastrophic events that befell the Jewish people

24. *b. Bava Metzia* 59b.

(such as the destruction of both temples and the Shoah), will show this to be true.

But let me be clear about what I mean by history. History is more than a series of data points. Those who record history as it unfolds—or who seek to unravel it based on artifacts and ancient texts—are rarely unbiased. The victor records his version of events, frequently leaving the vanquished without a voice. This seems particularly true with the history of the Jewish people, and I believe the talmudic rabbis understood this.[25] Their discussions of history seek out a balance of sorts, at times portraying events with hyperbole to underscore the magnitude of Jewish suffering and at other times infusing these same events with theological meaning in an attempt to make them comprehensible.[26] In the next section, we will therefore undertake an examination of this rabbinic history, with the goal of understanding the theological underpinnings they gave to key events. This will require a detailed analysis of various biblical and talmudic texts, along with commentaries to both. What it won't involve is either an explanation of or a rationalization for these events, in particular the Shoah.

In anticipation of this analysis, it is worth asking, What do we hope to learn from it? A major underlying assumption of the biblical canon is that God is just and His ways are just. Indeed, God Himself acknowledges this when He gives His rationale for discussing the fate of Sodom with Abraham. "For I have known him [Abraham] because he commands his sons and his household after him, that they should keep *the way of the Lord to perform righteousness and justice.*"[27] Bolstered by their unflappable faith in God's justice, the three friends are convinced that Job sinned. Had he not, Job's suffering would have been both unjust and impossible. Job categorically denies that he has sinned, and the simple reading of the text seems to support this. Job argues that suffering exists among people separate from sin, and the Shoah at the very least shows this to be true.[28]

---

25. Helfgot, "Unlocking the Riddle," 3 n. 10, suggests "that in the non-halakhic sections of the Bible, the rabbis of the midrash were not presenting traditions dating back to Sinai. They were engaging in exegetical, homiletical and, at times, even polemical interpretations of the text that do not always reflect the plain sense of the verses."

26. See n. 12 above.

27. Gen 18:19.

28. There are those who maintain that the Shoah happened as a result of the rise of Reform and other non-Orthodox forms of Judaism. For example, Satmar leader Rabbi Joel Moshe Teitelbaum once wrote: "Because of our sinfulness we have suffered greatly, suffering as bitter as wormwood, worse than any Israel has know since it became a

people. . . . In former times, whenever troubles befell Jacob, the matter was pondered and reasons sought—which sin had brought the troubles about—so that we could make amends and return to the Lord, may He be blessed. . . . But in our generation one need not look far for the sin responsible for our calamity. . . . The heretics have made all kinds of efforts to violate these oaths, to go up by force and to seize sovereignty and freedom by themselves, before the appointed time. . . . [They] have lured the majority of the Jewish people into awful heresy, the like of which has not been seen since the world was created. . . . And so it is no wonder that the Lord has lashed out in anger. . . . And there were also righteous people who perished because of the iniquity of the sinners and corrupters, so great was the [divine] wrath" (Ravitzky, *Messianism*, 124). Then there is the example of Rabbi Ovadia Yosef, the former Sephardi chief rabbi of Israel and a highly respected *posek* (halakhic authority), who was quoted in the Israeli press in 2000 as saying that six million Jews perished in the Shoah because they were reincarnations of sinners. They are "reincarnations of the souls of sinners, people who transgressed and did all sorts of things that should not have been done. They have been reincarnated in order to atone" (Reeves, "Holocaust Victims").

Others contend that Zionism was the sin that caused the Shoah, as the Jews should have waited for the Messiah rather than proactively try to build a Jewish state in Palestine. An interesting twist on this appears in the writings of what some call redemptionist Zionists, who also saw the Shoah as a collective punishment for a collective sin: ongoing Jewish unfaithfulness to the land of Israel. Rabbi Mordecai Atiyah was a leading advocate of this idea. Rabbi Zvi Yehudah Kook and his disciples, for their part, avoided this harsh position, but they, too, theologically related the Shoah to the Jewish recognition of Zion. Kook writes, "When the end comes and Israel fails to recognize it, there comes a cruel divine operation that removes [the Jewish people] from its exile" (Ravitzky, *Messianism*, 124).

Some Jewish thinkers have rejected the traditional responses to human suffering, as well as the notion of Jewish complicity through their sins, in favor of more original responses. Both Eliezer Berkovits and Arthur A. Cohen adopt the "free will" defense, which states that humans have free will to do as they please, whether good or evil, and thus it is not God but human beings who caused or even allowed the Shoah. Unlike Berkovits and Cohen, Emil Fackenheim does not remove God from the Shoah. In effect, he places God at the scene of the crime itself—Auschwitz—but says that he cannot understand exactly what God was doing there. Whatever God's intention, Fackenheim believes that the Shoah should be considered a new occasion of divine revelation and that a proper response to it is the adoption of a 614th Jewish commandment: not to allow Hitler a posthumous victory by letting Judaism die out (Shoah Resource Center, "Jewish Philosophical and Theological Responses to the Holocaust").

In contrast, most Modern Orthodox Jews reject the idea that the Shoah was God's fault or the fault of the Jewish people themselves. Modern Orthodox rabbis such as Joseph Ber Soloveitchik, Norman Lamm, Abraham Besdin, Emanuel Rackman, Eliezer Berkovits, and others have written on this issue, and many of their works have been collected in Rosenberg and Heuman, *Theological and Halakhic Reflections*. These rabbis are not the only ones to reject the idea that the Nazis' victims were sinners. The Lubavitcher Rebbe, for one, vigorously rejected this view, as he stated: "The destruction of six million Jews in such a horrific manner that surpassed the cruelty of all previous generations could not possibly be because of a punishment for sins. Even the Satan himself could

Nevertheless, I believe that the Jews have historically sided with the friends. In the face of suffering, the Jewish people seemingly always search for the sin behind it, no matter how righteous the person.[29] We need only look to the rabbinic views concerning the experiences of the Jewish forefathers to see the extent to which this is done.

The midrash relates that Jacob was so righteous that an image of his face was engraved on God's heavenly throne.[30] Yet our rabbis at times "blame" Jacob for bringing suffering upon himself. As the verse says, "Yaakov dwelt in the land of his father's sojournings, in the land of Canaan."[31] Reflecting the rabbinic tradition, Rashi poignantly comments, "When Yaakov sought to dwell in tranquility, the troubles of Yosef sprang upon him. The righteous seek to dwell in tranquility. Said the Holy One, blessed be He, 'What is prepared for the righteous in the world to come is not sufficient for them, but they seek [also] to dwell in tranquility in this world!'"

Even Jacob himself is fearful of his shortcomings. For example, as he prepares to face his brother Esau after a twenty-year separation, he says: "O God of my father Avraham and God of my father, Yitzhak, the Lord, Who said to me, 'Return to your land and to your birthplace, and I will do good to you.' I have become small from all the kindnesses and from all the truth that You have rendered Your servant, for with my staff I crossed this Jordan, and now I have become two camps."[32] Commenting on the words "I have become small," Rashi explains Jacob's fears as follows: "My merits have diminished [that is, become small] because of the kindnesses and the truth that You have rendered me. Therefore, I fear lest I have become sullied with sin since [the time that] You promised me, and it will cause me to be delivered into Esav's hand[s]."

Then there is Joseph, called *ha-tzaddik* (the righteous one) in talmudic literature. Clearly his path was laid out by God, as he rose from a simple shepherd in Canaan to become, as it were, the COO of the most powerful nation in the world. He saves Egypt and the Jewish people from the ravages of famine. He is lauded for resisting the temptation of Potiphar's wife. He is praised for being the same Joseph throughout his life—be he slave or

---

not possibly find a sufficient number of sins that would warrant such genocide!" (*Sefer HaSichot* 5751, 1:233).

29. See Besdin, "Holocaust," 137–38.

30. *Gen. Rab.* 82:2.

31. Gen 37:1.

32. Gen 32:10–11.

head of state—and for never hiding the fact that he is a Jew.[33] Yet there is a tradition that his sufferings were *middah ke-neged middah*, that is, measure for measure. In other words, he brought suffering upon himself. How so? At the onset of his amazing and trying experiences, Joseph is introduced as follows:

> These are the generations of Yaakov: when Yosef was seventeen years old, being a shepherd, he was with his brothers with the flocks, and he was a lad, [and was] with the sons of Bilhah and with the sons of Zilpah, his father's wives; and Yosef brought evil tales about them to their father.[34]

The commentators are all curious. What are these "evil tales" that Joseph brings to his father about his brothers? Relying on rabbinic tradition, Rashi emphasizes the extent to which Joseph's suffering was rooted in his own actions.

> Any evil he saw in his brothers, the sons of Leah, he would tell his father: that they ate limbs from living animals, that they demeaned the sons of the handmaids by calling them slaves, and that they were suspected of illicit sexual relationships. For these three [tales] he was punished: For [the report that his brothers ate] limbs from living animals, "they slaughtered a kid" (Gen 37:31); when they sold him and did not eat it alive. For the report that he told about them that they called their brothers slaves, "Yosef was sold as a slave" (Ps 105:17); and concerning the illicit sexual relationships that he told about them, "his master's wife lifted her eyes, etc." (Gen 39:7).

Even as he later languishes in prison, the rabbis see Joseph as being punished with two additional years because of his sins.[35] Why? Why not

---

33. The midrash (*Deut. Rab.* 2) explains that the one who acknowledges Israel as his land deserves to be buried there, whereas he who does not do so will not be buried there. When Potiphar's wife called Joseph an *ish 'ivri* (a Hebrew), Joseph did not deny it and later stated that he came from the land of the *'ivrim* (Gen 40:15). In contrast, when the daughters of Jethro reported that they were saved by Moses and identified him as an *ish mitzri* (an Egyptian), Moses did not correct them. Therefore, he did not merit burial in the land of Israel.

34. Gen 37:2.

35. Rashi on Gen 40:23 states: "Because Yosef relied on him to remember him, he was compelled to be confined for two years, as it is said: 'Praiseworthy is the man who made the Lord his trust and did not turn to the haughty (רְהָבִים)' (Psalms 40:5). He did not turn to the Egyptians, who are called רַהַב, haughty."

concede that Joseph's experiences and suffering were simply part of God's plan and that they are beyond our understanding?[36]

Let me suggest an answer. It seems clear that the rabbis are uncomfortable with the notion of the righteous suffering. It violates their worldview, one in which God is just and His ways are just. Thus, to give meaning (or to try to give meaning) to seemingly random tragedies and misfortunes, to explain the suffering of the righteous, the rabbis seek to infuse tragedy and suffering with meaning, and more often than not, this entails blaming the victim. How else does one make sense of rabbinic interpretations of the trials and tribulations of Joseph or his father Jacob or even of Job?

As for me, I freely confess my inability to fully comprehend God's ways, but this does not impinge on my faith. As a rabbi, I believe that God is just. I also believe that people perceive injustice in the world, some of which they believe to come from the divine. I'm not quite sure where the line is between incomprehension and injustice, but I also believe that we should not stand passively by in the face of perceived injustice and accept it. We should challenge it and God, too, if we somehow think Him to be unjust. This may seem to be a contradiction for people of faith, but isn't this exactly what Abraham did when he kept coming back to God to challenge Him about the fate of Sodom? Wasn't each interim step Abraham proposed to God still an injustice in Abraham's eyes?[37] As Abraham ultimately says to God, "Far be it from You! Will the Judge of the entire earth not perform justice?"

Job learns from the example of Abraham. God's whirlwind diatribe forces (or as some would say, bullies) Job into admitting there is much in the world he does not understand, but like Abraham, he will not suffer injustice silently. He cannot if he, like all of us, is to be an empowered partner in completing creation. This is why he calls God "dust and ashes," that is, he will not accept as an answer the fact that man cannot fully understand the world and God's actions when faced with a perceived injustice.[38]

---

36. There are, of course, commentaries that explicitly make this point, among them *Netivot Shalom*, which maintains that the entire saga of Joseph is beyond our ken.

37. Gen 18:20–33.

38. I am not alone in suggesting that man will not and cannot fully accept God's actions in the face of perceived injustice or extreme suffering. Rabbi Kaloxylos Kalmish Shapiro, the last Chasidic rebbe of Eastern Europe, perished in the Warsaw Ghetto. Yet his weekly Torah discourses, which he put in a manuscript entitled *Eish Kodesh* ("Sacred Fire"), somehow survived. In 1939, he spoke of and analyzed the verses in the Torah which deal with the death of Sarah. He quotes Rashi, who states that Sarah's soul fled and

Intuitively, I believe that my understanding of *dust and ashes* is not only plausible but a much-needed rereading of Job. Yet, as one whose approach to biblical scholarship is text-based, I need more than intuition. And so I propose examining the circumstances surrounding the destruction of the temples and the Shoah to see if they lend legitimacy to my reading of *afar va-eifer*. Before doing so, I would like to return once again to that modern Job, Elie Wiesel, to see how one can navigate between the ashes of God and of life.

We have seen how Wiesel describes his soul and dreams turning to ash. This is a theme he returns to throughout his novel *Night*. "This day [Rosh Hashanah 1944] I ceased to plead. I was no longer capable of lamentation. On the contrary, I felt very strong. I was the accuser, God the accused. My eyes were open and I was alone—terribly alone in a world without God and without man. Without love or mercy. *I had ceased to be anything but ashes*, yet I felt myself to be stronger than the Almighty, to whom my life had been tied for so long."[39]

I don't know if Job felt himself at the end of his saga to be stronger than God, but he, like Wiesel, survived his ordeals, not unblemished, not whole, but willing to continue life's struggles. Neither man, despite their sufferings, despite the accusations each hurls at God, walks away from God. This is critically important for our understanding of Job and for the analysis we are about to undertake of the Shoah and the destruction of both temples.

The convergence between the book of Job and my questions regarding the founding of the modern state of Israel should be growing clearer. Up to this point, our extensive textual analysis of an obscure point of grammar has suggested an alternative reading of the end of the book of Job, namely, that Job refers to God as "dust and ashes." I believe that a similarly detailed

---

she died upon being told of the binding of Isaac. Rabbi Shapira then offers this remarkable insight, one that lends support to our reading of *afar va-eifer*: "So Moshe our teacher, the trusted shepherd, deliberately edited the Torah. He placed these two events—the death of Sarah and the binding of Yitzhak—side by side in the text in order to advocate on our behalf. By doing this, Moshe is suggesting that if the anguish is, God forbid, unbearable, then death can result. . . . The Torah may also be telling us that our mother Sarah, who took the binding of Yitzhak so much to heart that her soul flew out of her, died for the good of the Jewish people. She died in order to show God that a Jew should not be expected to suffer unlimited levels of anguish" (Shapira, *Sacred Fire*, 14). Is there any doubt that Rabbi Shapira, without using our expression "empowered partner," sees Sarah as such? Indeed, Job merely resorts to words to challenge God. In Rabbi Shapira's view, Sarah gives her life to make her point.

39. Wiesel, *Night*, 54; emphasis added.

examination of the rabbinic literature that deals with the Jewish people's exile from their homeland will show that this alternative reading both makes great sense and has significant theological implications. Although this was not my original intent in studying the book of Job, undertaking this analysis also brought me much closer to answering my previously unanswerable question regarding the restoration of Jewish sovereignty in the land of Israel.

Yet, even as we delve into history (albeit the rabbis' perspective on this history), we must not overlook important textual sources, for the two—text and history—are ever present in my search for answers.

A defining characteristic of Jewish sages is their ability and willingness to search for a hopeful or redemptive outcome even in the face of the most dire circumstances. A quick perusal of chapter 9 of the talmudic tractate *Berachot* illustrates this. Several mishnayot in this chapter discuss which blessing a person must say upon hearing good news or upon hearing bad news. One mishnah goes on to conclude that a person must say a blessing upon hearing good news and upon hearing bad news, regardless of whether the actual outcome was positive or negative.[40] A second mishnah posits that a person must bless God both for positive things that happen to him or her and for negative things.[41] The Sages explain that this latter mishnah refers not to a specific blessing a person must actually say but rather to the manner in which a person should accept events that happen in his or her life. Even if they are negative, a person should still accept them with happiness.[42]

What is the source for reciting blessings on good and bad alike? These mishnayot rely on Deut 6:5: "And you shall love the Lord, your God, with all your heart, with all your soul and with all your might." In the words of the Mishnah, "With all your heart means with both your inclinations, the evil as well as the good; with all your soul means even should He deprive you of life; and with all your might means with all your property." In comparison, the Tosefta provides a different source for this same dictum. "Rabbi Meir says: From where [do we know] that just like you have to bless [God] for good [things that happen to you], so too you have to bless [God] for bad

---

40. "Man is bound to say the blessing for evil without reference to the good that may accrue from it; and for good without reference to the evil that may accrue from it" (*b. Berakhot* 9:3).

41. "Every man is bound to bless God for evil, as well as he is bound to thank him for [the] good [he receives]" (*b. Berakhot* 9:5).

42. *b. Berakhot* 60b.

[things that happen to you]? The Torah teaches us, '... that which Hashem, your God, has given you' (Deut 26:11). Your God [meaning] your judge. For every judgment that He judges you, whether positively or negatively."[43]

Though these mishnayot help explain the inclination of the Sages to seek out hope and look for the positive, there is another possible source for their worldview. Darkness is a common metaphor for evil and despair, whereas light is an often-used symbol for goodness and hope. The order of creation has darkness preceding light. When there is but darkness in the world, it is a place of astonishing emptiness and, one could say, of hopelessness. Only with the creation of light does God characterize His creation as "good."[44] Thus, the very order of creation hints at the notion that goodness inevitably emerges from darkness and that hope must always prevail over despondency.[45]

The rabbinic propensity for anticipating and searching for reasons to be hopeful colors many aspects of Jewish life and ritual. For example, when the Sages instituted a weekly reading from the Prophets in response to the Roman ban on public Torah readings, they were careful to choose texts that ended on a positive note.[46] Even the most distressing of the texts designated by the rabbis for public reading, the book of Lamentations, has an additional verse appended to it. Rather than closing with the disheartening final verse of the book, "For if You have utterly rejected us, You have [already] been exceedingly wroth against us,"[47] the reader and the congregation conclude the public reading by reciting aloud the more uplifting verse, "Restore us to You, O Lord, that we may be restored! Renew our days as of old."[48]

What does all this have to do with Job and, more specifically, with our efforts to prove that Job is referring to God with his use of the phrase *afar*

---

43. *t. Berakhot*, chapter 6, tosefta 3. In the printed editions of the Tosefta the word "Meir" is missing and the text instead reads "Rabbi," which is a general reference to Rabbi Yehudah Ha-Nasi, the editor/compiler of the Mishnah. However, all manuscripts have the text written as "Rabbi Meir."

44. Gen 1:2–4.

45. *Netivot Shalom* discusses this idea repeatedly in its commentary to the Torah.

46. Serious Roman persecution of the Jews began c. 135 CE. Jews were forbidden, upon pain of death, from practicing many rituals, including circumcision, public reading of the Torah, and eating unleavened bread at Passover. Moreover, a temple dedicated to the Roman god Jupiter was erected during this period on the Temple Mount in Jerusalem. A temple of Venus was also built on Golgotha, just outside the city.

47. Lam 5:22.

48. Lam 5:21.

va-eifer? A great deal, actually. The rabbinic inclination toward optimism and hope, combined with the rabbis' decision to include the book of Job in the biblical canon, makes reconciliation between Job and God inevitable. This is neither surprising nor unexpected, for only reconciliation can turn the darkness of Job's suffering into something positive and enduring, and this in turn justifies its inclusion in the Bible.

Inevitable or not, Job achieves a reconciliation with God only after his final speech. Job utters a few short sentences (which include the problematic *dust and ashes*), and God immediately chastises the three friends for not speaking correctly, "as did My servant Job" (42:7). He goes on to restore Job's health. He grants him great wealth: "fourteen thousand flocks and six thousand camels and a thousand yoke of cattle and a thousand she-donkeys" (42:12). He blesses him with fourteen sons and three daughters. Clearly, given the immense and frequent sufferings of the Jewish people over the millennia, it would have been in our best interests to internalize the lessons of Job and to replicate his conciliatory speech as often as possible.

Yet, what part of this speech should the Jewish people have emulated?

According to the traditional understanding of this speech and of the term *afar va-eifer*, emulating Job would have entailed the Jews' humbling themselves before God and acknowledging that there is much in His ways that is simply beyond understanding. This would have been particularly appropriate subsequent to the great national catastrophes suffered over the centuries by the Jewish people. However, if we study the history of this people, especially in the aftermath of the destruction of the First and Second Temples, it is hard to see any Jobian influence consistent with the traditional reading of the end of the book in Jewish responses to these events. Conversely, Jewish responses to the Shoah seem to be different, and I would argue that this difference can and should be explained in the context of our proposed understanding of *dust and ashes*. I hope to show (and thus answer my unanswerable question) that the restoration of Jewish sovereignty over the land of Israel is a direct result of the Jewish people no longer seeing themselves as *afar va-eifer* but instead coming to see God as such.[49]

49. For many, the reasons why God chose the previous generation to reestablish the state of Israel remain shrouded in mystery, and among those who suggest possible explanations, most credit God, not the Jewish people, with this miraculous event. Perhaps Joseph Ber Soloveitchik summed it up best when he wrote, "The establishment of the State of Israel is a contemporary example of God's intervention to an undeserving generation. Although previous generations of Jewish leadership were spiritually exalted, Hashem saw

I recognize that this is a bold claim, but it is one I believe a careful analysis of both history and various biblical and rabbinic texts will support. Before launching into this analysis, it will be important to delineate the similarities and some critical differences between Job and the Jewish people.[50] With these in hand, we will proceed to examine three seminal events in Jewish history: the destruction of the First Temple in 586 BCE; the destruction of the Second Temple in 70 CE; and the destruction of European Jewry by the Nazis during the years 1939–1945. We will consider when and why the Jewish people returned to the land of Israel and when and why they remained in exile. By doing so, I believe we will see that history supports our reading of *afar va-eifer* in Job as referring to God, just as it will support the notion that the establishment of the modern state of Israel should be seen as a logical outcome of the Jewish people taking this same position vis-à-vis God. If so, this will answer my questions about the events of 1948 and the establishment of the modern state of Israel.

---

fit to bestow the State of Israel to our generation, in an age of religious and moral midgets, as it were. The reason may be that earlier generations did not need a State of Israel for their Judaism to survive. Ezekiel was able to experience God in exile, in a concentration camp in Babylonia. In contrast, without a State of Israel today, many among the Jewish people would be lost in a tidal wave of assimilation" (Lustiger, *Before Hashem*, 100–101).

50. See n. 3 above.

CHAPTER 5

God, Job, and the Jewish People

BEFORE BEGINNING TO EXAMINE the three aforementioned seminal events in Jewish history, a few remarks regarding the connection between Job and the Jewish people are in order.

There is an obvious and fundamental difference between Job and the Jewish people. Whereas Job is free of sin (notwithstanding the accusations of the three friends to the contrary), various biblical and rabbinic texts portray the Jewish people as sinning often and repeatedly during the years leading up to the destruction of both the First and Second Temples.[1] Hence, the Jewish people cannot argue, as did Job, that their suffering postdestruction was arbitrary. However, they could have—and I believe should have—argued that the *magnitude* of their suffering approached the unjustifiable. In this respect, namely, that the magnitude of their suffering is unjustifiable, the Jewish people have a commonality with Job.

A second important difference involves how and when God communicates with Job and with the Jewish people. God did not forewarn Job of his impending suffering. In fact, messenger after messenger appear suddenly to Job to announce, while "this one was still talking," yet another calamity that has befallen his family. In comparison, God repeatedly warns

---

1. We can make such statements based on the admonitions and warnings delivered by the prophets to the Jewish people on behalf of God prior to both destructions (the books of Isaiah and Jeremiah are excellent examples). This we dare not do vis-à-vis the Shoah, for given the absence of prophetic warnings prior to the Nazis' destruction of European Jewry, an assumption of guilt on the victims' part would create a causality we can neither prove nor, in my view, justify.

the Jewish people prior to the destruction of both temples of the consequences of their sinful activities. It is not surprising that God is prepared to speak to a community (even a non-Jewish one[2]), in advance of punishing it for sinful behavior, in a way He is unwilling to do with individuals. As various biblical texts demonstrate, God warns the Jewish people through the beginning of the Second Temple period. In part, God's warning is a reflection of the great mercy and compassion He has for all creation, as He explains to Jonah: "Now should I not take pity on Nineveh, the great city, in which there are many more than one hundred twenty thousand people who do not know their right hand from their left, and many beasts as well?"[3] In part, it also reflects the special relationship He has with the Jewish people, one based on the covenant He made with Abraham and reaffirmed at Sinai.[4] Given this, God, if we can say such a thing, has no choice but to forewarn the Jewish people, and we will return below in greater detail to this type of communication between the people and God.

There are some similarities between Job and the Jewish people that are every bit as obvious and noteworthy as their differences. In the course of their suffering, both lose everything—property, home, family. Yet both wish to maintain a relationship with God. Job articulates this clearly. "Behold, let Him kill me, I will hope for Him; but I will prove my ways to His face" (13:15).[5] So, too, do the Jewish people, with a plea recited to this day every time a Torah scroll is returned to the ark. "Restore us to You, O Lord, that we may be restored! Renew our days as of old."[6] In each case, suffering

---

2. This is exactly what he did with the great non-Jewish city of Nineveh: "And the word of the Lord came to Yonah son of Amittai, saying 'Arise, go to Nineveh, the great city, and proclaim against it, for their evil has come before Me'" (Jonah 1:1–2).

3. Jonah 4:11.

4. Exod 19:3–6: "So shall you say to the house of Jacob and tell the sons of Israel, You have seen what I did to the Egyptians, and [how] I bore you on eagles' wings, and I brought you to Me. And now, if you obey Me and keep My covenant, you shall be to Me a treasure out of all peoples, for Mine is the entire earth. And you shall be to Me a kingdom of princes and a holy nation."

5. Rashi explains this verse as follows: *Behold, let Him kill me*: I will not separate from Him, and I will always hope for Him. Therefore, there is no rebellion or transgression in my words, but I will reason to His face about my way and my character traits with which I have conducted myself, to know of what He will find me guilty."

6. Lam 5:21. Even Elie Wiesel, that Joblike figure who wrote so poignantly of his soul being murdered and his dreams being turned to dust, confesses his yearning for God though the pain of the Shoah lingers. As he explains, "I never divorced God. I couldn't. I'm too Jewish. . . . I cannot live without God" (Wiesel, "Interview").

(even when deemed unjustifiable by those who experience it) does not and cannot extinguish longing for a positive and loving relationship with God. Nonetheless, in each case the path to reconciliation with God meets with differing degrees of success. And the key to success? The cause for failure? To me, it all comes down to how one uses *afar va-eifer*.

Let us now begin our analysis of both the First and Second Temple periods. This will involve several stages, and we will assume that the reader is familiar with the events that preceded the destruction of each temple. Those who are unfamiliar with these events or who would like to review them should consult the appendices to this essay.

First, we will examine the warnings given to the Jewish people, both in the Torah and in the prophetic writings, which foretold the dire consequences should they stray from the service of God. Specifically, this will include a close look at the *tochachot*, that is, the admonitions in the Torah in which God spells out in great detail the punishments that would befall the Jewish people and which Nachmanides[7] interprets as applying specifically to the periods in question, being sure to consider the extent to which the *tochachot* were fulfilled.

Second, we will carefully review the prophetic warnings conveyed to the Jewish people to gain a better understanding of the transgressions of the nation. As a complement to this, we will also engage in a detailed analysis of various talmudic texts in which the rabbis set forth their understandings of the people's transgressions to ascertain if and why the rabbinic enumeration differs from that of the prophets.

Finally, we will consider, through a Jobian filter, the Jewish people's reconciliation (or lack thereof) with God during the postdestruction periods, in an effort to establish whether the historical record lends support to our understanding of the phrase *afar va-eifer*.

One caveat is in order before beginning our analysis. We generally tend not to speak of the timeline of the Jobian narrative, and even if we did, it would be measured in weeks and months. In comparison, the timeline of the temples' destruction covers centuries. Moreover, we examined the Jobian narrative through the exegetical lens of a single text. In considering the destruction of both temples, we must consider a broad array of texts,

7. Rabbi Moshe ben Nachman (b. 1194, d. 1270), also known as Nachmanides or the Ramban, was perhaps the greatest Torah scholar of his era. He has also been described as one of history's first Zionists because he declared that it is a *mitzvah* to take possession of Israel and to live in it. Acting on his own words, Nachmanides moved to the Holy Land during the Crusades, after he was expelled from Spain for his polemics.

including biblical, rabbinic, and even contemporaneous works (such as those of Josephus and Dio Cassius). Despite these differences, the end goal remains the same, namely, uncovering Job's intent in uttering the phrase *afar va-eifer*.

The midrash tells us that "there are seventy faces to the Torah—turn it around and around, for everything is in it."[8] In other words, the Torah is a layered and nuanced text, and as such, there is no single way to examine and understand any given biblical verse or verses. This is particularly true for the *tochachot* (*tochachah* in the singular). They appear twice in the Torah, first in Lev 26 and again in Deut 28. Both are much debated. Why do these warnings appear twice in the Torah? Are they predictive (that is, declaring that the Jewish people *will* sin) or speculative (that is, *if* they sin, these will be the consequences)? Why are they stylistically so different? How is it that the second *tochachah* was delivered independently by Moses?[9]

Many have wrestled with these and similar questions. One contemporary scholar, Haskel Lookstein, in explaining the difference between the two, observes that God uses the first *tochachah* to establish His covenant with all of Israel.[10] What was the context for this covenant? When the second set of *luchot* (stone tablets brought down from Mount Sinai by Moses) was delivered to replace the first (which Moses had broken upon witnessing the people worshipping the golden calf[11]), the people themselves called for a new oath to be administered. Although Moses delivered the words, God is considered to have administered the oath Himself to the entire Jewish people, including Moses. In contrast, the second *tochachah*, the one set forth in Deuteronomy, concludes, "These are the words of the covenant . . . besides the covenant that was executed with [the Jewish people] at Chorev."[12] This, too, represents an oath between the Jewish people and God, one in which the people affirm that they will observe the Torah in its entirety. This time, however, Moses makes the covenant, one-on-one as it were, with each member of the Jewish people. Though he may have been divinely inspired to do so, Moses is considered to be the administrator of the oath.

---

8. *Num. Rab.* 13:15.

9. Abaye points out in *Mesechet Megillah* that the first *tochachah* is in the plural and is delivered by Moses from the mouth of God, whereas the second *tochachah* is in the singular and is delivered by Moses on his own.

10. Lookstein, "Parshat Ki Tavoh."

11. Exod 32:15–19.

12. Deut 28:69.

Lookstein notes another critical difference between the two *tochachot*. The contents of the first *tochachah* are fierce, sharp, and awesome yet end with words of hope, consolation, and encouragement. Redemption will come. Despite the harshness, there will be a bright future. The *tochachah* in Deuteronomy is radically different. There is, in Lookstein's words, no happy ending.

This is an important difference, one that is critical to our understanding of *afar va-eifer*. Lookstein, based on the work of Soloveitchik, suggests that an answer can be gleaned from the commentary of Nachmanides on the *tochachot*. I agree. Nachmanides examines the *tochachot* in great depth and is a frequently cited source for unraveling their meaning. His may not be the only approach, but it is one that resonates with me and seems to make the most sense. More important, it will, I believe, advance our analysis of *afar va-eifer*.

Nachmanides develops in detail the notion that the two *tochachot* refer to two different periods. The first, he maintains, refers to the destruction of the First Temple and the subsequent Babylonian exile. The second in his view predicts the conditions surrounding the fall of the Second Temple at the hands of the Romans. Nachmanides seeks to prove his thesis by looking at the different punishments in the two *tochachot*. For example, one verse in the first *tochachah*, "Then the land shall make up for its Sabbaths,"[13] refers to the Babylonian exile. How so? The seventy years of exile between the two temples parallel the seventy *shemittah*[14] years that the talmudic rabbis maintain were not kept during the First Temple period.[15] This verse thus

13. Lev 26:34.

14. *Shemittah*, the sabbatical year, is the seventh year of the seven-year agricultural cycle mandated by the Torah for the land of Israel. Torah law dictates that during the seventh year all agricultural activity—including plowing, planting, pruning, and harvesting—cease. Its observance was considered by the rabbis to be a test of religious faith.

15. *Seder Olam* is an often-cited source for this point. Based on it, Rashi explicitly writes on Lev 26:35 as follows: "The seventy years of the Babylonian exile correspond to the seventy years of sabbatical years and jubilees [which were neglected], and [thus] were years during which Israel angered God in their land—four hundred and thirty years. Three hundred and ninety were the years of their sin, from [the time] they entered the land until the Ten Tribes went into exile. And the inhabitants of Yehudah angered Him forty years from [the time] the Ten Tribes went into exile until the destruction of Yerushalayim—as it is said in [the Book of] Yechezkel (4–6): 'Lie on your left side, etc. [When] you complete these, you will lie on your right side [again]'—'forty days'—you will bear the iniquity of the House of Judah.' This prophecy was said to Yechezkel in the fifth year of the exile of King Yehoyochin, and they lasted yet another six years until the exile of King Tzidkiyohu—which yields [the number] forty-six. And if you say Menasheh's

lays out a justification for the exile. In contrast, the second *tochachah* is seemingly predictive when it states, "God will scatter you among all the peoples from one end of the Earth to the other end of the Earth."[16] This appears to forecast Titus's taking the captives of Israel and dispersing them in many countries, keeping the younger ones captive and leaving their elders to weep, as it says, "Your sons and daughters shall be given to another people, and your hand will be powerless."[17]

It is clear from these examples that Nachmanides considers some parts of the *tochachot* to be predictive and other parts to be speculative or justificatory in nature (that is, they explain why the people deserve these consequences). Identifying the extent to which each of the *tochachot* fits into these classifications will help with our overall analysis, and this will require a careful and close reading both of the text and of Nachmanides's commentary thereon. Let us thus proceed.

It is important to note that the admonitions set forth in the first *tochachah* are preceded by a series of promises in which God assures the people that He will reward them for observing His laws and statutes.

> If you follow My statutes and observe My commandments and perform them, I will give your rains in their time, the Land will yield its produce, and the tree of the field will give forth its fruit. Your threshing will last until the vintage, and the vintage will last until the sowing; you will eat your food to satiety, and you will live in security in your land. And I will grant peace in the Land, and you will lie down with no one to frighten [you]; I will remove wild beasts from the Land, and no army will pass through your land; You will pursue your enemies, and they will fall by the sword before you; Five of you will pursue a hundred, and a hundred of you will pursue ten thousand, and your enemies will fall by the sword

years were fifty-five, [I would answer] Menasheh repented for thirty-three years, and all the years of his wickedness were twenty-two—as they (the Rabbis) said in the *Aggadah* of *Chelek* (Sanhedrin 103a)—and [those] of Amon: two, eleven for Yehoyochin, and similarly for Tzidkiyohu. Go calculate for 436 years the [number of] sabbatical years and jubilees contained in them, they [number] 16 [years] per century—14 sabbatical years and 2 jubilees—resulting in 64 [years] for four centuries, [and] for 36 years [we have] five sabbatical years—[the total] is seventy minus one. [There is] yet another year, for [this 436-year period] ended with a sabbatical year, which completes the seventy. And on them (the Israelites) was decreed [an exile] of seventy complete years, and so [the verse] says in Divrei Hayomim II (36, 21), 'until the land had paid her Sabbaths, etc. to fulfill her seventy years.'"

16. Deut 28:64.
17. Deut 28:32.

before you. I will turn towards you, and I will make you fruitful and increase you, and I will set up My covenant with you. You will eat very old [produce], and you will clear out the old from before the new. And I will place My dwelling in your midst, and My Spirit will not reject you; I will walk among you and be your God, and you will be My people.[18]

In reflecting on these promises, Nachmanides, like the talmudic rabbis before him, views them through both historical and theological filters. He sees miracles brought about by the hand of God where skeptics and those lacking in faith instead see myth or mere coincidence. Nachmanides thus confidently writes that "all these blessings are miracles, for it is not natural that the rains should come [in their due season] and that we should have peace from our enemies and that they should have faintness of heart so that a hundred of them flee before five as a result of us observing the statutes and commandments of God."[19] To him, these are hidden miracles, brought about by "the natural events of the world occurring according to their habit."[20] Nonetheless, each is mentioned separately because of their constant and continuous occurrence in the land and for the people. This principle will serve as a lynchpin to Nachmanides's entire theological approach to the *tochachot*, for he maintains that "when Israel is in perfect [accord with God], constituting a large number, their affairs are not conducted at all by the natural order of things, neither in connection with themselves, nor with reference to their Land, neither collectively nor individually, for God blesses their bread and their water and removes sickness from their midst, so that they do not need a physician and do not have to observe any of the rules of medicine."[21] The converse would thus seem to be equally true, that is, when the Jewish people are not "in accord with God," the consequences will not be "conducted at all by the natural order of things." This would seem to explain (theologically and perhaps even historically) some of the events we will shortly examine surrounding the destruction of the First Temple, such as stones burning and mothers eating the carcasses of their dead babies.

This, of course, begs the question (to which we already know the answer). These promised blessings were clearly conditional: "If you follow My

18. Lev 26:3–12.

19. Nachmanides, *Commentary*, 3:460.

20. Ibid.

21. Ibid., 3:461.

statutes and observe My commandments and perform them." Nachmanides acknowledges that the Jewish people never attained or earned them, either as a nation or as individuals. Yet he insists that they "will be fulfilled for us at the time of [our] perfection."[22] What, then, has kept the Jewish people from achieving this "perfection"? Nachmanides notes that the first *tochachah* begins with the phrase "if you despise My statutes and reject My ordinances."[23] He highlights the fact that statutes are commandments for which an underlying rationale has not been revealed. They are and ought to be observed for no other reason than that God has commanded us to do so. As such, argues Nachmanides, only fools reject them. Ordinances, however, are laws that everyone desires and needs, for without them "there can be no civilized life for any people or country."[24] This is why, explains Nachmanides, the verse states, "if you despise . . . ," for only one who "despises" these ordinances will reject and not keep them.

In this context, God uses the first *tochachah* to specifically list the statutes the people rejected (and thus seemingly despised) during the First Temple era, including (according to Nachmanides) the high places on which they offered forbidden sacrifices, sun-images, and idols.[25] This would explain why God states, "I will lay your cities waste and make your holy places desolate, and I will not partake of your pleasant fragrances."[26] Nachmanides sees in this verse a warning from God to the Jewish people that He will remove His sanctuary from among them and that He will no longer accept their offerings (which He had previously favored). He also understands it as providing a basis for the punishments that God will subsequently bring down upon the Jewish people: the sword,[27] wild beasts,[28]

---

22. Ibid., 3:465.

23. Lev 26:15.

24. Nachmanides, *Commentary*, 3:465.

25. Lev 26:30.

26. Lev 26:31.

27. "I will bring upon you an army that avenges the avenging of a covenant, and you will gather into your cities. I will incite the plague in your midst, and you will be delivered into the enemy's hands" (Lev 26:25).

28. "I will incite the wild beasts of the field against you, and they will bereave you, utterly destroy your livestock and diminish you, and your roads will become desolate" (Lev 26:22).

pestilence, famine,[29] and, finally, exile.[30] Significantly, Nachmanides maintains that the things delineated in these verses happened and were later recorded in the book of Jeremiah. "Thus He warned them and thus it happened."[31] In this manner, Nachmanides reconciles history and theology.

Does accepting Nachmanides' premise that the first *tochachah* describes circumstances surrounding the destruction of the First Temple mean that the Jews were destined to sin? Or did the admonitions simply spell out what would happen in the event the Jews were to sin?

These are important theological questions, but they do not impact our efforts to ascertain a true understanding of *afar va-eifer*. In hindsight, we know (as recounted in the Bible and affirmed by the rabbis) that the Jewish people sinned, and this differentiates them from Job. They further differentiated themselves from Job by seeming to adopt the position of Job's friends, namely, that suffering is and must be the result of sin. Let us turn to the prophetic revelations that preceded the destruction of the First Temple, in particular those of Ezekiel and of Jeremiah, to see how accurately the *tochachah* foretold events and the magnitude of the sins underlying those events.

In September 592 BCE, Ezekiel was taken to Jerusalem "in visions of God" that revealed to him the terrible, idolatrous state of the temple. He also witnessed the departure of the Shekhinah, the divine presence, in stages from the temple.[32] In 587 BCE, Ezekiel's young wife died, a sign from God that Jerusalem was about to fall.[33] The prophet was not allowed to mourn her passing, and this was intended to be a warning to the Jewish people. "And you shall do as I have done; you shall not enwrap yourselves over your upper lip, and you shall not eat the bread of men. And your glory [shall be] on your heads and your shoes on your feet; you shall neither lament nor weep, and you will melt because of your iniquities, and you will moan one to the other."[34] The symbolism here is explained by Rashi: "You shall not observe mourning because you have no consolers, for none

---

29. "When I break for you the staff of bread, and ten women will bake your bread in one oven, and they will bring back your bread by weight, and you will eat, yet not be satisfied" (Lev 26:26).

30. "And I will scatter you among the nations, and I will unsheathe the sword after you. Your land will be desolate, and your cities will be laid waste" (Lev 26:33).

31. Nachmanides, *Commentary*, 3:468.

32. Ezek 10–11.

33. Ezek 24:16–18.

34. Ezek 24:22–23.

among you is not a mourner, and there is no mourning except where there are consolers."

Whereas Ezekiel accompanied a large group of exiles to Babylonia, the prophet Jeremiah (627–580 BCE) remained in Jerusalem during the final siege and destruction. At times, Jeremiah seemed to view God's judgments toward the people of Judah as personal judgments directed toward him, and in the end God did not allow him to pray for the people.[35] For forty years, Jeremiah continued to preach and warn the people, all without any reward or sense of accomplishment. He specifically predicted both the destruction of Jerusalem and the subsequent seventy years of exile and captivity, a prophecy that will figure prominently in our analysis. He also pronounced judgment on Babylonia.

> "And the whole land shall be a desolation and an astonishment, and these nations shall serve the king of Babylonia seventy years. Then it will come to pass, when seventy years are completed, that I will punish the king of Babylonia and that nation, the land of the Chaldeans, for their iniquity," says the Lord; "and I will make it a perpetual desolation."[36]
>
> For thus says the Lord: "When seventy years are completed for Babylonia, I will visit you, and I will fulfill to you my promise and bring you back to this place. For I know the plans I have for you, says the Lord, plans for welfare and not for evil, to give you a future and a hope. Then you will call upon me and come and pray to me, and I will hear you. You will seek me and find me; when you seek me with all your heart, I will be found by you, says the Lord, and I will restore your fortunes and gather you from all the nations and all the places where I have driven you, says the Lord, and I will bring you back to the place from which I sent you into exile."[37]

The actual destruction of Jerusalem (generally dated to 586 BCE) and severe suffering of its inhabitants are graphically described by Jeremiah in the book of Lamentations. His sorrow-laced words echo the destruction that Nachmanides argues is clearly foretold in the *tochachot*.

To this point, we have examined the predictions of the events (as well as the events themselves) surrounding the destruction of the First Temple. We will now consider various talmudic sources in which the rabbis discuss

---

35. Jer 8:16.

36. Jer 25:12–13.

37. Jer 29:10–14. Babylon was subsequently judged and leveled as predicted. In 553 BCE, Babylon fell to the Medes and the Persians (see Dan 5).

and debate the sin (or sins) that sealed the fate of the Jewish people and led to their exile. In the texts that follow, various Sages offer reasons for the destruction of Jerusalem and of the First Temple. At first glance, one might conclude that these Sages disagree with one another, as each seems to cite a specific and unique cause for the city's destruction. However, the Maharsha[38] maintains that the subsequent opinions cited in the text do not contradict the first opinion mentioned but instead comment on different aspects of Jerusalem's destruction.[39]

> Abaye said: Jerusalem was destroyed only because they desecrated the Shabbat in it; as [the verse] states: "[Her Kohanim have done violence to my Torah . . .] and from My Sabbaths they averted their eyes and I became profaned in their midst."[40]
>
> R' Abahu said: Jerusalem was destroyed only because they neglected to recite the Shema[41] mornings and evenings; for [the verse] states: "Woe [to] those that rise early in the morning [and] pursue old wine, [that linger late into the night [till] wine inflames them.]"[42] And it is written [in the next verse there]: "And the harp and the lyre, the drum and the flute and the wine, are their parties; but to the works of Hashem they do not look."[43] And [in the next verse] it is written: "Therefore my people have gone into exile for want of knowledge."[44]

38. Samuel Eidels (1555–1631), famous for his commentary on the Talmud, *Chiddushei Halachot*, is also known as Maharsha, a Hebrew acronym for "Our Teacher, the Rabbi Shmuel Eidels."

39. *b. Shabbat* 119b.

40. Ezek 22:26. Although Israel is called to task for many sins in that passage, the chapter concludes, "Therefore I have poured out my anger against them, with the fire of My wrath I have consumed them" (Ezek 22:31). As the Maharsha explains, since the destruction described is by fire, Abaye concludes that this was the underlying cause for Jerusalem's destruction.

41. The Shema is a centerpiece of Jewish worship, and its first verse sums up the monotheistic core of Judaism: "Hear, O Israel: the Lord our God, the Lord is one" (Deut 6:4). Observant Jews consider it to be one of the most important parts of their prayer service and view its twice-daily recitation as a religious commandment.

42. Isa 5:11. As Rashi explains, they spend their mornings and evenings drinking and partying when they should be reciting the Shema.

43. According to Rashi, they pay no attention to their obligation to proclaim God's unity to his creations for they are too busy pursuing their pleasures.

44. That is, for their failure to recognize the importance of saying the Shema. The commentators to the verse (Targum, Rashi, and Radak) explain the phrase "but to the works of Hashem they do not look" as referring to the failure to spend time studying Torah. Had the people studied Torah in place of pursuing good times, they would have

Rav Hamnuna said: Jerusalem was destroyed only because they diverted the school children in it [from their Torah studies]; as [the verse] states: "[to] pour [fury] on little children in the streets etc."[45] What is the reason that [fury will] pour out? Because little children are in the street [instead of in the classroom where they belong.][46]

Ula said: Jerusalem was destroyed only because they had no shame for each other; as [the verse] states: "They should have been ashamed, for they committed an abomination; yet they are not at all ashamed etc."[47]

R' Yitzchak said: Jerusalem was destroyed only because the great and the small were considered equal; as [the verse] states: "And it shall be as with the people so with the Kohen" and [immediately] afterwards it is written: "The land will be utterly emptied."[48]

Rav Amram the son of R' Shimon bar Abba said in the name of R' Shimon bar Abba [who] said in the name of R' Chanina: Jerusalem was destroyed only because they did not admonish one another; as [the verse] states: "Its leaders were like harts that found no pasture."[49] Just as this hart [walks in a herd with] the head of this one next to the tail of that one, so too did the Israelites of that generation bury their faces in the ground [to avoid seeing the wrongdoing around them], and they did not admonish one another.[50]

---

learned what God expected of them and would have been able to avert destruction. Instead, their indulgence in wine and song blinded them to the doom that awaited them, and the exile came upon them for lack of knowledge.

45. Jer 6:11. The full text of the verse is: "I am filled with [prophecies of] the fury of Hashem, I am weary of bearing them; [to] pour out [this fury] onto little children in the streets and onto the gatherings of youths together."

46. As the Maharal explains, when the young are not educated in the Torah, it is the beginning of the end for a Torah society. The destruction of the future soul of the society therefore brings about its physical destruction.

47. Jer 6:15. In the view of the Maharsha, had a sense of shame at least been preserved many would have held back from committing various offenses for fear of being caught and humiliated.

48. Isa 24:2. As the Maharsha explains, a society that does not esteem greatness will cease to produce truly great people. Thus, even its teachers and sages will be flawed and devoid of true Torah greatness.

49. Lam 1:6.

50. The significance of the analogy should be obvious. Just as the hart walking in this formation sees no more than the tail of the animal in front of it and is thus oblivious to what may be happening to any other part of the lead animal, so, too, with the leaders of

Rav Yehudah said: Jerusalem was destroyed only because they demeaned Torah scholars in it; as [the verse] states: "But they mocked the messengers of God, despised His words and scoffed at His prophets, until the wrath of God rose up against His people, until there was no remedy."[51]

And Rava said: Jerusalem was destroyed only because people of truth had disappeared from it; as it says: "Search in the open places of Jerusalem and see now and know and seek in its streets if you will find a man, if there is one who dispenses justice, who seeks the truth—and I will forgive her."[52]

In a second talmudic source, in the context of a discussion regarding the frequent turnover of high priests during the Second Temple era, we find a comparison of that period to the First Temple era. Among the questions pondered as part of this comparison was this: Why was the First (or Second) Temple destroyed? Unlike the previous source we examined, which brought a multitude of possible reasons for the destruction of the First Temple, this talmudic text is relatively concise and to the point.[53]

Why was the First Temple destroyed? Because of three [iniquitous] things that existed there—idolatry, immorality and bloodshed.[54]

---

that generation. They made it a point not to look too closely at what their colleagues were doing so as not to have to criticize them.

51. 2 Chr 36:16. The last chapter of Chronicles recounts the last years of the monarchy and Israel's destruction at the hands of the Babylonians. In it, the prophet gives God's reasons for destroying the land and the temple. The verse just before the one quoted by Rav Yehudah states: "And Hashem, the God of the fathers, sent to them at the hands of His messengers, early and repeatedly, because He had compassion on His people and on His dwelling place." The verse cited by Rav Yehudah continues, "But they mocked the messengers . . . ." This was the final sin that caused God's anger to pour out against His people: the fact that they mocked the prophets that He, in his mercy, had sent to lead them back to the proper path. As the Maharsha notes, once the sinner has fallen to the level of mocking those who are sent to save him, there is no longer any hope for him.

52. Jer 5:1. Rav Ketina challenges Rava's statement and brings textual proof that people of truth did not disappear from Jerusalem even in the hour of its downfall. Ultimately, the Gemara resolves this dispute, concluding that the verses cited by Rav Ketina referred to matters of Torah, in which people were indeed truthful even in the city's final hours, whereas the verses cited by Rava referred to business matters, an area full of corruption and lacking in people of truth. This explains why, in the verse cited by Rava, the prophet Jeremiah says to "search in the open places of Jerusalem . . . and seek in its streets [for an honest man]," for the dishonesty to which he referred was the dishonesty of the marketplace.

53. *b. Yoma* 9b.

54. In Judaism, these are the three cardinal sins, transgressions so grave that one

Idolatry as it is written: "for the couch is too short for stretching out, and the cover too narrow for curling up."[55] What is the meaning of "for the couch is too short for stretching out?" R' Yonasan said: This couch [the Temple] is too short for two companions to have dominion over it at one time.[56] [And what is the meaning of] "and the cover is too narrow for curling up?" R' Shmuel bar Nachmani said: Whenever R' Yonasan would come to this verse, he would weep. He would say: "He [God] of Whom it is written, "He gathers like a mound the waters of the sea,"[57] has an idol become a rival to Him?

After demonstrating that idolatry existed in the time of the First Temple, the talmudic text goes on to cite sources demonstrating that the other two cardinal sins, immorality and bloodshed, were also prevalent during the First Temple era.

Immorality, as it is written: "Hashem said: Because the daughters of Zion are haughty, walking with outstretched necks and with gazing eyes, floating as they walked, and with their feet they would spew venom."[58] "Because the daughters of Zion are haughty," [this means] that a tall woman would walk next to a short woman.[59] "Walking with outstretched necks," [this means] that they would walk with erect posture. "And with gazing eyes," [this means] that they would fill their eyes with makeup [and beckon to the young men].[60] "Floating as they walked," [this means that] they would walk [with short steps, putting the] heel [of one foot] next to the big toe [of the other].[61] "And with their feet they would spew venom." R' Yitzchak said: They would take myrrh and balsam, place them in their shoes [and walk in the marketplaces of Jerusalem], and

---

must sacrifice one's life rather than commit them (b. Sanhedrin 74a).

55. Isa 28:20.

56. That is, the temple cannot house the divine presence and an idol at the same time. One or the other must go. Rashi understands this verse to refer to the idol that King Menasseh installed in the temple (2 Kgs 21:70).

57. Ps 33:7.

58. Isa 3:16.

59. The implication of the verse is that they did something to make themselves appear taller than they actually were. Hence, the Gemara's comment that a tall woman purposely walked next to a short woman to enhance her attractiveness.

60. See b. Shabbat 62b, along with Rashi's accompanying commentary.

61. That is, they would walk slowly, as if floating, so that men could stare at them.

when they reached unmarried Jewish youths,[62] they would stamp [on the ground] and spray [the perfume] over them, driving the Evil Inclination into them like the venom of an angry [snake].[63]

Bloodshed, as it is written: "Moreover, Menasheh shed very much innocent blood, until he filled Jerusalem with blood from end to end."[64]

They were wicked people but they placed their trust in the Holy One, blessed be He. We have come to [the period of the First Temple].[65] As it is written, "Her heads judge for bribes and her priests issue rulings for a fee and her prophets divine for money, yet they rely on Hashem, saying 'Is not Hashem in our midst? Nothing bad will befall us!'"[66] Therefore the Holy One, Blessed is He, visited upon them three decrees corresponding to the three sins in their hands,[67] as the verse states: "Therefore, because of you, Zion shall be plowed as a field, and Jerusalem shall become ruins, and the Temple Mount [shall be] as the high places of the forest."[68]

---

62. The fact that the text refers to unmarried men is seen by Rashi (when taken together with the text from *b. Shabbat* 62b, discussed in the next note) as an indication that the women visiting the market are married. Thus, the verse alludes to adulterous behavior.

63. This entire back-and-forth is repeated verbatim in the name of Rava the son of Rav Ilai in *b. Shabbat* 62b. There the discussion continues and considers the punishments that will befall such women. Moreover, after discussing the haughtiness of the women of Jerusalem, the discussion turns to the men. The men are found to be as haughty as the women, and Rav Chisda specifically deduces that the questions the men asked one another, although seemingly discreet (such as, "Did you recline on a wide couch or a narrow couch?"), all pertained to illicit sexual relations. Taken together, these two talmudic sources make clear that adulterous behavior was very much present during the First Temple period.

64. 2 Kgs 21:16. The Gemara in *b. Sanhedrin* 103b says this refers either to Manasseh's murder of the prophet Isaiah (which was a crime so heinous that it was, according to Rashi, as if Manasseh had filled Jerusalem with blood from end to end) or to the daily murder of many men by forcing them to carry a crushingly heavy idol.

65. That is, this is a proper depiction of the people who lived during this time. Despite their wicked deeds, they trusted in God. In comparison, as we will see, the people of the Second Temple period did not, their Torah learning and observance of its commandments notwithstanding.

66. Mic 3:11.

67. That is, the three cardinal sins of idolatry, immorality, and bloodshed.

68. Mic 3:12. The point the Gemara is making here is that the Jews of the period were not guilty of apostasy, that is, of holding no law of the Torah sacred. Rather, they simply succumbed to one temptation after another even as they maintained their trust in God. As such, the three sins of this generation were treated by God as three separate wrongs

By demonstrating the existence of the three cardinal sins of idolatry, immorality, and bloodshed during the First Temple period, the talmudic sages seemingly came to grips with the theological basis for the exile of the Jewish people. They specifically held that idolatry, immorality and bloodshed are causes of exile.[69] But is this really so? I am not so sure. In fact, I believe that applying a Jobian filter to this talmudic analysis of the sins of the people during this period will yield very different insights into the hows and whys of the rabbis' debate.

Our entire purpose in applying a Jobian filter to the Jewish people's reconciliation (or lack thereof) with God during the postdestruction period and subsequent exile to Babylonia is to establish whether the historical record as understood by the rabbis lends support to our understanding of the phrase *afar va-eifer*. Before moving to this analysis, let us recall that there are two obvious and fundamental differences between the experiences of Job and those of the generation of the First Temple. First, Job did not sin, whereas the people of the First Temple did, and, by their own admission (or at least in the eyes of the talmudic sages), they did so repeatedly. Thus, the people cannot argue, as did Job, that their suffering was arbitrary. (Whether it was justified, that is, whether the punishment fit the crime, is a question we will turn to shortly.) Second, God did not forewarn Job of his impending suffering, whereas He did warn the people of Judah of the impending consequences of their sinful activities prior to the destruction of the First Temple.

Notwithstanding these differences, does the Jobian narrative work for the First Temple era? More specifically, does the return of the people from the Babylonian exile (and the subsequent restoration of the temple) conform to the traditional reading of Job? In other words, are the Jewish people restored as a result of a humble and contrite response on their part vis-à-vis their suffering, as is Job (according to the typical approach to the narrative) when he states that he despises (or abhors) himself and repents in dust and ashes?

At first glance, the answer would seem to be yes, but that first glance would at best be incomplete and is more likely incorrect. There are three reasons for this. The first involves the nature of God's relationship with the Jewish people. God is interchangeably portrayed in rabbinic literature and in ritual liturgy as both King and Father. In the face of repeated and

deserving of three separate punishments.

69. *b. Avot* 5:9.

continuous wrongdoing, the King should and did demand justice, and thus the Jewish people were deprived of the sacred abode of God's presence and were exiled from their land. Yet God the Father looks for grounds to be forgiving and merciful. He well knows that punishment cannot be avoided, but He opts to temper it and does so by spelling out in advance what this punishment will be and how long it will last.

> For thus says the Lord, that after seventy years of Babylon are completed, I will remember you and perform my good word concerning you to make you return to this place.[70]
>
> I, Daniel, considered in the books the number of years whereof the word of the Lord came to Jeremiah the prophet that he would complete seventy years of the ruins of Jerusalem.[71]

The Babylonian exile was, in the end, relatively short (especially in comparison to the Jewish people's second exile), but this brevity seemingly was not brought about by the actions of the Jewish people. Instead, it was the result of God playing the role of a good parent and laying out the consequences in advance for the misbehavior of His children.[72] Indeed, even if the Jewish people had been properly contrite (and they were not, as will be demonstrated below), their exile had to last seventy years, no more and no less, for that is what God had ordained.[73]

A second factor that argues against the notion that the Jewish people were redeemed from exile as a result of their humility and contrition is the very nature of this restoration. The incomplete nature of the restoration is hinted at in the first *tochachah*. As Nachmanides notes, God only assures Israel "that He will remember the covenant of the fathers and of the remembrance of the Land, but not that He will forgive their iniquity and their sin and that He will once again love them as of old. . . . Nor does

---

70. Jer 29:10.

71. Dan 9:2.

72. Child psychologists, classical and contemporary alike, see this as a preferred method for disciplining wayward children. ("Jimmy, if you do that you'll go to time-out for 5 minutes. . . . Sally, if you continue with that behavior you'll lose your computer privileges for the rest of the day.") See, for example, Skinner, *Science and Human Behavior*, and Barkley and Benton, *Your Defiant Child*.

73. It is worth noting that rabbinic tradition maintains that the non-Jewish kings of this period dreaded the climax of the seventy years, and each in turn attempted to determine when these years would end.

He state that they will return to Him in complete repentance, but only that 'they shall confess their iniquity, and the iniquity of their fathers.'"[74]

A more explicit proof is found in the rabbis' comparison of the two periods preceding the destruction of the two temples. Though they ultimately conclude (as we will see) that the underlying theological causes for the destruction of both temples were very different, the rabbis search for additional differences between the two epochs. They specifically note that gratuitous hatred brought about the destruction of the Second Temple but question its existence during the First Temple period.[75]

> Was there no gratuitous hatred in [the period of] the First Temple? But it is written: "[Cry out and wail, Son of Man! For it was among My nation, it was among the prices of Israel.] Fearers of the sword were My people, therefore smite upon your thigh [in grief]."[76] And R' Elazar said: [This verse refers to] those people who eat and drink together but stab each other with the daggers of their tongue.[77]
>
> That was [true only] in regard to the princes of Israel as it is written: "Cry out and wail, Son of Man! For it was among my Nation, [it was among the princes of Israel]." And it was taught in a *Baraita*[78] [concerning this verse]: "Cry out and wail, son of Man!" One might think [that one should wail] for everyone [because the sin of gratuitous hatred was prevalent then among all the people. Therefore] Scripture teaches: "It was among the princes of Israel [alone]."[79]

Having made the point that gratuitous hatred was a sin prevalent only in the Second Temple period, the text continues with its comparison of the two eras, focusing on the relative merits of both generations and inquiring if and how these merits influenced the restoration of the First Temple (and the lack of restoration of the Second Temple).

---

74. Nachmanides, *Commentary*, 3:468.

75. *b. Shabbat* 119b.

76. Ezek 21:17.

77. That is, to speak evil of one another. Thus, we see that unwarranted hatred did exist during the period of the First Temple.

78. *Baraita* designates a tradition in Jewish oral law not incorporated into the six orders of the Mishnah. Nevertheless, these "outside" works are frequently used by the Talmudic sages as prooftexts in their analysis and interpretation of the Mishnah.

79. Since baseless hatred was limited to the leaders of Israel and was not prevalent among the general population, it could not have been the cause of the destruction of the First Temple.

R' Yochanan and R' Elazar both said: The earlier ones whose iniquity was revealed[80] had their end revealed;[81] the later ones whose iniquity was not revealed,[82] their end was not revealed.

R' Yochanan said: The fingernail of the earlier [generations] was better than the [entire] abdomen of the latter ones.[83] Reish Lakish said to him: On the contrary, the later ones are better [because] even though [they] are [subjected to the] dominion of [foreign] kingdoms, they occupy themselves with [the study of] Torah.[84] [R' Yochanan] said to him: The [presence and absence of the] Temple demonstrates [that the earlier generations were superior] for [the Temple] was restored to the earlier ones but it has not [as yet been] restored to the later ones.[85]

Notwithstanding the views of these Sages, the notion that the First Temple period was greater than that of the Second Temple is premised largely on the degree to which the divine presence was said to be evident in both eras. Indeed, this explains the response of Rabbi Elazar to his peers when they ask which was greater. His response? "Set your eyes upon the Temple."[86] The people and buildings of both periods may have been

80. According to Rashi, they transgressed Torah laws openly and made no effort to conceal their wrongful behavior.

81. Jeremiah prophesied that the Babylonian exile would end in seventy years, and so it did.

82. The Maharsha explains that they harbored unwarranted hatred toward their fellow men in their hearts even while they would eat and drink together publicly in a congenial manner.

83. Again, according to the Maharsha, the implication is that the most trifling member of the earlier generations is superior to the most distinguished member of the later generations.

84. Although the earlier generations rose to greater heights than the later generations, they did so under conditions that were more conducive to spiritual elevation. The later generations lived under conditions that were ill suited to the study of Torah and observance of mitzvot, due to constant harassment from their Gentile rulers and renegade Jews who threw their lot in with the Gentiles. Yet, despite all the adversity, they strived for spiritual elevation. Based on the principle set forth in *b. Avot* 5:23 that "the reward is in proportion to the exertion," Reish Lakish concludes that the achievement of the later generations was even greater. One can only speculate to what extent Reish Lakish's earlier life experiences (he was said to have been both a bandit and a gladiator prior to become one of the most prominent sages of the second generation) influenced his view on this matter.

85. *b. Shabbat* 119b.

86. Ibid. Interestingly, the Jerusalem Talmud in *Yoma* 1:1 states that only the roof was destroyed at the time of the First Temple's destruction, whereas the entire edifice

outwardly similar, but they differed in significant ways. According to rabbinic tradition, the divine presence was visibly discernible in the temple compound throughout the First Temple period, and prophets regularly brought the word of God to the people. When the people would ascend the Temple Mount, they would see ongoing miracles reflecting the revelation of God, including the pillar of God's glory and the fire that descended from heaven to consume the sacrifices.[87] The land could not be destroyed and its people exiled until the divine presence removed itself from the people.

The three cardinal sins—idolatry, immorality, and murder—were seen by the talmudic sages as the epitome of impurity.[88] When the people of the First Temple period immersed themselves in these sins, their temple became unfit as the domicile of the Divine. This explains why God's presence deserted it, and a temple without the divine presence is a hollow shell, waiting to crumble. Thus, the people and their temple were primed to fall before the onslaught of Nebuchadnezzar.

The third point militating against the idea that the Jewish people were redeemed because of their response to the exile is far more nuanced than the previous two. Applying the traditional reading of Job (that is, that he saw himself as dust and ashes) to the events up to and after the destruction of the First Temple assumes that the Jews were humble and contrite before God, and this would seem to be what drives the rabbis' discussions of the people's many sins. In fact, one could argue that the breadth and detail of the talmudic discussions we have quoted to this point reflect the attitude of the Sages (as codified by Maimonides in the first chapter of his *Laws of Repentance*) that one who confesses and expounds upon his sins as part of repentance is to be greatly praised. Yet, I do not think that this is what the

---

was razed at the time of the destruction of the Second Temple. This would suggest that the sins at the time of the Second Temple were more serious. This same source goes on to say that any generation in which the temple is not rebuilt is considered as if it had destroyed it.

87. *m. Avot* 5:5 gives the complete list of these miracles: "No woman ever miscarried because of the smell of the holy meat. The holy meat never spoiled. Never was a fly seen in the slaughterhouse. Never did the High Priest have an accidental seminal discharge on Yom Kippur. The rains did not extinguish the wood-fire burning upon the altar. The wind did not prevail over the column of smoke [rising from the altar]. No disqualifying problem was ever discovered in the Omer offering, the Two Loaves or the Showbread. They stood crowded but had ample space in which to prostrate themselves. Never did a snake or scorpion cause injury in Jerusalem. And no man ever said to his fellow 'My lodging in Jerusalem is too cramped for me.'"

88. *b. Shevu'ot* 7b.

Sages were striving for when they enumerated sin after sin leading to the destruction of the First Temple. I believe that they were prepared to accept the loss of the temple and even of their land because of the extent to which their sins ruptured their relationship with God. What they could not accept was the idea that any sin, any wrongdoing, could justify the magnitude of the suffering described by the prophet Jeremiah.

> Even the jackals offer the breast and suckle their young; the daughter of my people has become cruel, like the ostriches in the wilderness. The tongue of the suckling child cleaves to his palate through thirst; the young children beg for bread, but no one breaks it for them. Those who used to eat dainties are perishing in the streets; they that were reared on crimson clasp the dunghills. The iniquity of my people is greater than the sin of Sodom, which was overthrown as in a moment, and no hands fell on her. Her Nazirites were purer than snow, they were whiter than milk, their appearance was ruddier than coral, and sapphire was their form. But now their appearance has become darker than charcoal, they are not recognized in the streets; their skin is shriveled on their bones; it has become as dry as a stick. Better off were the victims of the sword than the victims of hunger, for they ooze, pierced by the fruits of the field. The hands of compassionate women boiled their own children; they have become their food in the destruction of the daughter of my people.[89]

I believe that the rabbis in the above-cited talmudic texts were not examining the possible sins of the Jewish people out of a sense of contrition but rather were searching for a justification for the magnitude and severity of their suffering. In essence, they were forced to attribute the misdeeds of the Jewish people to the three cardinal sins because only sins of this magnitude would make "the punishment fit the crime."[90] And why were they forced to do so? Because they could not bring themselves, as we would have Job do, to view God as dust and ashes.

Where does this leave us? How does this analysis help resolve our questions about *afar va-eifer*? The truth is, it doesn't. It is not that the Jews

---

89. Lam 4:3–10.

90. Maimonides, in the fifth chapter of *Hilchot Yisodei Hatorah*, points out that the Torah commands the Jewish people to live by its statutes and that this is interpreted by the Sages to mean that if given the choice between violating one of the commandments of the Torah or being killed, a Jew should choose violation over death. However, this principle does not apply to the three cardinal sins. Without exception, a Jew must willingly sacrifice him- or herself rather than violate one of these three grievous sins.

of the First Temple period did not "get" Job or did not understand his final speech. It's just that his story was irrelevant to their circumstances. This is because their exile was to end after seventy years, irrespective of whether they saw themselves or God as dust and ashes. It was simply what God decreed. More important, their response (contrite or otherwise) was clearly lacking, for as we have also demonstrated, their restoration was incomplete. The Second Temple paled in comparison to the First. In contrast, no matter how one understands Job's final speech, his health and wealth were fully restored. Whatever the intent of his *dust and ashes*, it apparently was what God wanted to hear.

We had hoped to establish a link between the response of the Jews of the First Temple and their restoration so as to glean some insight into the true intent of Job's response to God at the end of that narrative. There is none, and thus, the events surrounding the destruction of the First Temple argue neither for nor against our understanding of *afar va-eifer*.

Our analysis of the Second Temple period will follow the same structure as that of the First Temple. We will assume that the reader is familiar with the events leading up to the destruction of the Second Temple, and those who are unfamiliar with these events should consult the appendices. Hence, our study of these events will begin with the *tochachot* and then move on to the prophetic warnings transmitted to the Jewish people prior to their exile. We will then examine the talmudic texts in which the rabbis grapple with the implications of the Second Temple's destruction. Last, we will once again consider through a Jobian filter the Jewish people's reconciliation (or lack thereof) with God during the postdestruction period. Whether the historical record of this era as established by the rabbis resolves the issue of how to interpret the phrase *afar va-eifer* in a way that the record of the First Temple did not remains to be seen.

The second of the *tochachot* appears in the book of Deuteronomy, and Nachmanides believes that it clearly alludes to what he terms "our present exile."[91] He is also convinced that this *tochachah* predicts that the Second Temple will not be as great as the First, and in this respect, the biblical text anticipates the talmudic debate on this very topic.[92] Last, Nachmanides sees

---

91. Nachmanides, *Commentary*, 3:468.

92. Nachmanides notes that this *tochachah* does not mention either the sanctuary or "the pleasing odor" of the offerings because the heavenly fire did not come down and consume the offerings that were brought to the Second Temple.

in this *tochachah* obvious references to the ultimate conquerors of the Jewish people of the Second Temple era, namely, the Romans.

> And He further states there among the imprecations, "The Eternal will bring a nation against you from far, from the end of the earth, as the vulture swoops down,"[93] alluding to the coming upon them of the Romans, who were very far from them. Thus, He states there, "a nation that you have not known; a nation whose tongue you shall not understand,"[94] because of their great distance from our Land. Such is not the case concerning the words of this covenant [i.e., the first of the *tochachot*], for [it speaks of the time when] they were exiled to Babylon and Assyria, which are near to our Land, and they always warred with them; and the stock of Israel comes from there, and they [the Jews] knew their language. . . . Again, He stated, "And the Eternal shall bring you back into Egypt in ships,"[95] and this happened in our [present] exile, when Titus filled the ships with them [captives]. . . . Similarly, that which Scripture says there, "Your sons and your daughters shall be given unto another people and your eyes shall see; You shall beget sons and daughters, and they shall not be yours, for they shall go into captivity"[96]—these are not references to the [Babylonian] exile, when both fathers and sons were exiled, but refer to that captivity of the sons alone [following the destruction of the Second Temple by the Romans], when the fathers remained in the Land. . . . Similarly, "Therefore shall you serve your enemy whom the Eternal shall send against you in hunger and in thirst"[97] is a reference to our servitude when we were subject to the Romans in our Land, and their officers ruled over us, pressing upon us a heavy yoke and taking away our people and our wealth, as is known in the [history] books.[98]

In comparison to what Nachmanides understands to be clear and obvious references to the exile of the Jewish people, the sins that will bring the exile about are, in his opinion, merely hinted at.

> We observe that He did not assure us of redemption, but He made it dependent upon our repentance. Neither did He mention among

93. Deut 28:49.

94. Deut 28:36.

95. Deut 28:64.

96. Deut 28:32, 41.

97. Deut 28:48.

98. Nachmanides, *Commentary*, 3:470–71.

the sins [for which they would be exiled that] they would make any Asherim and sun-images or that they would worship any idols whatsoever. Rather, He said, "But it shall come to pass, if you will not harken unto the voice of the Eternal your God, to observe to do all His commandments and His statutes,"[99] thus stating that because they will transgress some of His commandments and will not keep and observe of all them, they would be punished.[100]

Which of these commandments they transgressed and which they failed to observe is a question the talmudic sages will ultimately wrestle with, as we shall see below. Yet, for Nachmanides it was clear, this uncertainty notwithstanding, that these sins would result in the removal of the divine presence entirely from the land.

We have already seen that the talmudic sages linked the exile of the Jewish people following the destruction of the First Temple to the three cardinal sins of idolatry, immorality, and bloodshed. When they were once again left to ponder a temple's destruction and a second exile, the Sages seemingly assumed that the underlying cause could not be the same. Hadn't the people already seen the high price of the three cardinal sins? How then did the Sages explain the destruction of the Second Temple?

But the Second Temple—[we know] that the people occupied themselves with Torah, *mitzvot* ["commandments"] and acts of kindness—why was it destroyed? Because of the gratuitous hatred that existed there. This teaches you that gratuitous hatred is tantamount to [the] three [cardinal] sins of idolatry, immorality and bloodshed [put together].[101]

In order to definitively establish that gratuitous hatred brought about the destruction of the Second Temple, the Sages had to show, as we have previously discussed, that such hatred did not exist during the First Temple

99. Deut 28:15.

100. Nachmanides, *Commentary*, 3:469–70.

101. *b. Shabbat* 119b; *b. Yoma* 9b. Rashi notes that "gratuitous" hatred is that which is directed toward individuals who have not committed any action for which it would be justifiable to hate them. A more contemporary source, the Chofetz Chaim, opines that when the Gemara says the Second Temple was destroyed because of "gratuitous" or baseless hatred (which is, in the view of the Gemara, tantamount to idolatry, immorality, and bloodshed), the reference is not solely to hatred that one internalizes. It also refers to a hatred expressed through gossip and slander (referred to in Hebrew as *lashon hara*, literally, an evil tongue). This becomes even clearer as the talmudic text goes on to show that causeless hatred existed among the ruling class of the First Temple period, as demonstrated by the fact that they stabbed each other with the "swords of their tongue."

period. The reason why is clear. If it had existed, would it not have been grounds for the first exile, given that it is tantamount to the three cardinal sins?

Thus the question remains: What is it about gratuitous hatred that led the Sages to equate it with the three cardinal sins? Anticipating this question, a *midrash aggadah* in the Jerusalem Talmud asks: "How is it possible that in the generation of King David, where everyone—even the children—knew Torah, when they went out to war there were casualties, while in the days of King Achav,[102] a generation of idol-worshippers, when they went out to war they were always victorious?" The Gemara explains, "In the days of King David there was causeless hatred and informing. In the days of Achav, despite the fact that they were idol-worshippers, they were united among themselves, and hence they were victorious in war."[103]

Unity among the Jewish people is a religious imperative, and rabbinic literature is replete with references to its supreme importance. For example, the Sages teach that when a person prays on behalf of his comrade while also in need of that for which he prays, God will address his personal needs first, because the supplicant brings great pleasure to God through his love of his fellow.[104] In a similar vein is the well-known dictum of Rabbi Akiva stating that loving your fellow as yourself is *the* great principle of the Torah.[105] The Sages also teach the converse, that is, that God has no tolerance for one who sows disunity in the community through slander and gossip. God says, as it were, that He and the gossiper cannot dwell together in this

102. Shortly after the death of King Solomon, his kingdom split. His son Rehoboam remained king of the southern portion (which came to be known as Judah) and his challenger, Jeroboam, took control of the northern part (called Israel) and of the legendary ten tribes. During his reign, Jeroboam forcibly kept his people from traveling to Jerusalem (which was in the southern kingdom) to offer sacrifices to God. In the end, he led them away from monotheism. Jeroboam's dynasty lasted only two generations, as did the dynasty of his rival Baasha. Afterward, the country suffered from a war between generals (Zimri, Omri, and Tibni). Finally, Omri managed to secure the kingdom, and he moved its capital to Samaria. Omri's son Ahab stabilized the internal political situation, built a strong army, and boosted the economy by entering into an alliance with Sidon (in Lebanon), thereby opening Israelite trade to the entire Mediterranean basin. Ahab is best known for his frequent clashes with Elijah, the fiery prophet who challenged the king and his wife Jezebel and their worship of Baal. This contest of wills, culminating in the showdown at Carmel, is one of the most dramatic stories in the Bible (see 1 Kgs 18).

103. *y. Pe'ah* 1:1, 16a.

104. *b. Bava Qamma* 92a.

105. *y. Nedarim* 30b; *Gen. Rab.* 24:7.

world.[106] Indeed, God finds disunity among His people so distasteful that when it occurs, it also fractures the unity between Him and the people.

In biblical times, God would communicate this in a miraculous manner. How so? When God commands Moses to build an ark for the tablets he brought down from Mount Sinai, He gives very specific instructions regarding its cover.

> And you shall make two golden keruvim; you shall make them of hammered work, from the two ends of the ark cover. And make one keruv from the one end and the other keruv from the other end; from the ark cover you shall make the keruvim on its two ends. The keruvim shall have their wings spread upwards, shielding the ark cover with their wings, with their faces toward one another; [turned] toward the ark cover shall be the faces of the keruvim.[107]

According to the Sages, the two *keruvim* (cherubs) represent the pairing of God and the Jewish people. When God was pleased with His people, the *keruvim* faced each other; when not, they miraculously turned away from each other.[108] At times of national strife or disunity, the *keruvim* would also turn away from each other, for this disunity would displease God greatly.[109] And how would the people be aware of this? The talmudic text provides a simple answer. Three times a year, on each of the pilgrimage festivals, the curtain to the Holy of Holies would be pulled to the side so that all the people could see for themselves the current configuration of the *keruvim*.[110]

Given their understanding of the *keruvim*, it is not surprising that the Sages of the postdestruction period, when searching for the underlying cause of their suffering, would settle upon a sin as serious as gratuitous hatred, for only wrongdoing of such magnitude could result in yet another destroyed temple and yet another exile. For the rabbis, analysis was more than a theoretical discussion. They wanted to know which of their actions had led to this situation so that they could rectify them and thus try to bring about reconciliation with God. Significantly, they recognized that

---

106. *b. Arakhin* 15b.

107. Exod 25:18–20.

108. *b. Bava Batra* 99a.

109. *Netivot Shalom* has a beautiful discourse on this topic. See Sefer Netivot Shalom Al Torah Shmot, "Ve-dibarti itcha mei al ha-parochet mei-ben shnei ha-keruvim."

110. *b. Yoma* 54a.

appeasing God at this point in time, or even reconciling with Him, would be difficult, because the destruction of the temple had precipitated a decline in the Jewish people themselves.

> R' Pinchas ben Yair says: From the time the Temple was destroyed, *chaverim* [that is, Torah scholars and their followers] and high-born men have been ashamed.[111] And their heads have been covered [that is, they hide their faces in embarrassment and mortification] and men of merit have been impoverished [and have become inconsequential]. But strong-armed men and slanderers have triumphed, and there is none who seeks and none who beseeches and none who inquires. Upon whom can we lean? Upon our Father in Heaven!
>
> R' Eliezer the Great says: From the day the Temple was destroyed, [Torah scholarship decreased so that] scholars began to be like schoolteachers and schoolteachers like synagogue attendants and synagogue attendants like [unlearned] commoners and commoners became steadily more impoverished [in wisdom and observance], and there is none who inquires and none who searches. Upon whom can we lean? Upon our Father in Heaven![112]

All the same, the rabbis' desire for reconciliation remained so strong that they instituted mourning practices even before the destruction of the temple actually occurred.

> During Vespasian's campaign [the Sages] decreed a ban on grooms' wreaths [a coronet made of one of a variety of materials] and on the *iyrus* [a type of musical instrument]. During Titus' campaign, they decreed a ban on brides' wreaths and that no man may teach his son Greek. During the final campaign [which concluded in the destruction of the Temple], they decreed that a bride may not go forth in a canopy within the city. But our Rabbis [later] permitted a bride to go forth in a canopy within the city.[113]

After the destruction of the temple itself, additional mourning rituals were proposed. As can be seen in the discourse below, some were rejected

111. The Maharsha explains as follows: Social hierarchy had collapsed. As a result, fools and the poorly educated would ridicule Torah scholars for what the former considered excessive scrupulousness in adhering to biblical laws. Slaves and people of dubious parentage would taunt the highborn with innuendo concerning their own ancestry.

112. *b. Sotah* 49a–b.

113. *b. Sotah* 49a. The rabbis who permitted the bride's canopy were Rabbi Yehudah Ha-Nasi and his court. As the Gemara will go on to explain, they did so in the interest of modesty, which is better safeguarded if the bride is sheltered from the sight of passersby.

as impractical, but others were adopted and continue to be observed to the present time.

> Our masters taught: When the Temple was destroyed the second time, large numbers in Israel became ascetics, binding themselves neither to eat meat nor to drink wine. R. Joshua got into conversation with them and said, "My sons, why do you eat no meat and drink no wine?" They replied, "Shall we eat meat, which formerly was brought as an offering on the altar, now that the altar has ceased to be? Shall we drink wine, which formerly was poured as a libation on the altar, now that it is poured no longer?" He said to them, "If so, we should eat no bread, because the meal offerings have ceased." They said: "Perhaps we will manage with fruit."

"We should not eat fruit either, because the first fruits are offered no more." "Perhaps we will manage with other fruits.

He said: "Well, then, we should not drink water, because the rite of pouring water is no longer observed. [Since they had no answer] they kept silent. So he said to them, "My sons, come and let me advise you. Not to mourn at all is impossible, because the decree that the Temple be destroyed has been executed [and requires mourning]. But to mourn too much is also impossible, because we may not impose a hardship on the community unless the majority can endure it."

Therefore the Sages have ordained the following: A man may plaster his house, but he should leave a small space uncovered. A man who is preparing all that is needed for a feast should leave out some small ingredient. And if a woman is putting on all her ornaments, she must omit one of them. For it is said, "If I forget thee, O Jerusalem . . . let my tongue cleave to the roof of my mouth."[114] He who mourns for Jerusalem will merit seeing the renewal of her joy, as is said, "Rejoice ye with Jerusalem . . . join in her jubilation, all ye that have mourned for her."[115]

In sum, the inferiority of the Second Temple period was acknowledged by the talmudic sages and was evident from the diminished stature of the Second Temple compared to the First. Nonetheless, the people of this period had, at least initially, one important redeeming factor: their unity. Their temple, diminished though it may have been, served as a symbol of this unity, at least until the people became overwhelmed by gratuitous hatred for one another. Once they descended to petty bickering and hatred,

114. Ps 137:5–6.
115. Isa 66:10; *b. Bava Batra* 60b.

they forfeited their one claim to divine protection. This, in turn, resulted in the loss of their temple and their land. This exile, as we all know, would continue for nearly two thousand years.

So what happened? Unlike the people of the First Temple generation, who searched and searched for some sin that would justify their suffering, the Jews of this era quickly acknowledged their wrongdoing—gratuitous hatred—and the seriousness of it. Further, unlike the people of the First Temple, who were assured prior to their exile that redemption would come in a mere seventy years, this generation took nothing for granted. They proactively instituted what they hoped would be restorative measures even before the fall of the temple and increased these after its destruction. In essence, they responded to their suffering in accordance with the paradigm traditionally ascribed to Job, that is, they were humble and contrite. In the end, they conducted themselves as if they were dust and ashes in the eyes of God, but to no avail. Their exile would last for centuries.

To me, there would seem to be two possible explanations for God's apparent unresponsiveness: either their contrition and repentance was insincere or theirs was not the response God was after. I find the former to be unlikely, as observant Jews to this day pray three times daily for the restoration of the temple (and the relationship with God that it signifies). More likely, their response to suffering was misguided and misinformed. I believe that they failed to properly understand the import of Job's *afar va-eifer* and that a careful study of post-Shoah events will demonstrate this to be true.

CHAPTER 6

God, Job, and the Shoah

OF THE MANY MOVING passages in Elie Wiesel's *Night*, none resonates more powerfully within me or seems more fitting for our analysis of the destruction of European Jewry by the Nazis than the one cited in the epigraph to this volume:

> "Man raises himself toward God by the questions he asks Him," he was fond of repeating. "That is the true dialogue. Man questions God and God answers. But we don't understand His answers. We can't understand them. Because they come from the depths of the soul, and they stay there until death. You will find the true answers, Eliezer, only within yourself!"
>
> "And why do you pray, Moshe?" I asked him.
>
> "I pray to the God within me that He will give me the strength to ask Him the right questions."[1]

When it comes to the Shoah, there are no right questions, and even for those we dare ask, of either God or human, there are no answers we are capable of understanding. Historians have extensively documented the methods of the Nazis' efficient and murderous brutality, and it is certainly not my intent to try to delve into the reasons for the Shoah. Can we understand it any more than we understand the many tragic events that have befallen the Jewish people over the centuries? Dare we trivialize and minimize the sufferings of the Jews by ranking and categorizing them or by speculating as to why God chose those times and places to subject His people to

---

1. Wiesel, *Night*, 2–3.

such experiences? Perhaps Rabbi Besdin said it best when he wrote that "there cannot be any answer, explanation, of restitution for a tragedy of such dimensions."[2]

We cannot and should not seek to answer such questions. Instead, I propose to look at the aftermath of the Shoah and try to gauge the reactions of the survivors vis-à-vis God. Were they humble and contrite before God, as the traditionalists maintain Job was at the end of his narrative, or did they challenge Him, as I believe Job did when he called God *afar va-eifer*?[3] More important, can we make a connection between their reaction to collective suffering and the reemergence of Jewish sovereignty over the land of Israel in 1948?

In this respect, I hope to adopt the analytical construct of Soloveitchik, which he set forth in his monumental essay on the Shoah, "Kol Dodi Dofek: It Is the Voice of My Beloved That Knocketh."

> Woe unto the man whose suffering has not precipitated a spiritual crisis in the depths of his being, whose soul remains frozen and lacking forgiveness! Woe unto the sufferer if his heart is not inflamed by the fires of affliction, if his pangs do not kindle the lamp of the Lord that is within him! If a person allows his pains to wander about the vast empty spaces of the cosmos like blind, purposeless forces, then a grave indictment is drawn up against him for having frittered away his suffering. . . . Man is obliged to resolve not the question of the causal explanation of suffering in all of its speculative complexity but rather the question of the rectification of suffering in all of its halakhic simplicity. He does this by transforming fate into destiny, elevating himself from object to subject, from thing to person.[4]

Said differently, I hope to establish that the post-Shoah generation of Jews, like Job before them, said to God, "Enough, it is now You who have become like dust and ashes to us," and that by doing so, they transformed a tragic fate into a magnificent destiny.

---

2. Besdin, "Holocaust," 138.

3. As I have done throughout this book, I employ terms such as "the Jewish people" or, in this case, "they" in a very broad, collective sense. Admittedly, not every Jew challenged God in this way, just as not every Jew prayed over the centuries for the restoration of the Jewish homeland and of Jerusalem. Rather, I am here being consistent with my use of this rhetorical device.

4. Soloveitchik, "Kol Dodi Dofek," 57–58.

Yet, let's be clear about one critical point. Zionism, as a political and nationalistic movement, predates the Shoah by more than fifty years. (Appendix D, which sets out a brief history of Zionism and the key milestones in the establishment of the modern state of Israel, underscores this point.) It is thus not a matter of the survivors deciding to build a state in response to the Shoah. Rather, it a question of why God chose this moment, after nearly two thousand years, to restore the Jews' sovereignty over their historic homeland. In brief, we are at this juncture discussing theology, not history or politics.

There is an additional caveat that must be set forth prior to proceeding with this next phase of our analysis. We live in a twenty-four-hour digital age, one in which images and news reports on any tragedy are available almost instantly, no matter how distant the event. An important ancillary benefit of this is the existence of video archives, and these, in conjunction with the detailed testimonials of survivors, make the Shoah a very real event to those who study it, even though it has been more than sixty-five years since its end. The images we see and the firsthand accounts we read give the Shoah an impact—and create within us a revulsion—that we do not typically associate with the destruction of the First and Second Temples. This is a mistake. The Shoah was perhaps the most incomprehensible of these three national catastrophes. Whereas both Babylonia and Rome were putting down revolts,[5] Nazi Germany was bent on mindless and unprovoked genocide. Nonetheless, the former were as brutal and horrific in many respects as was the Shoah.[6]

5. See Appendices B and C for more details.

6. Two brief talmudic passages from *b. Gittin* 58a will illustrate the extent to which the rabbis employed hyperbole and exaggeration to underscore their theological view of these events:

"R' Chiya bar Avin said in the name of R' Yehoshua ben Karchah: One elderly resident of Jerusalem told me that in this valley, Nevuzaradan, the chief [Babylonian] executioner, slaughtered two hundred and eleven myriads [i.e., 2,110,000 people] and in Jerusalem on one stone he slaughtered ninety-four myriads [i.e., 940,000 people].... R' Assi said: Four *kavs* [the volume of 96 eggs] of brains [of young children whose skulls had been smashed upon it] were found on one stone. Ulla says: Nine *kavs* [the volume of 216 eggs].

"Rav Yehudah said in the name of Shmuel who said in the name of Rabban Shimon ben Gamliel: There were 400 synagogues in the city of Bethar [during the period prior to the destruction of the Second Temple] and in each and every one there were 400 teachers of children and before each and every [teacher] there were 400 students. When the enemy entered [the city], [the students] stabbed them with their sticks. But when the enemy prevailed and captured [the students] they wrapped [the students] in their scrolls and set them on fire."

Of the three national catastrophes we have considered, the Shoah is without doubt the most Jobian. Like Job, the victims of the Shoah had no warning.[7] There was no prophet beseeching the people to repent. Like Job, the Jews did not sin, or at least not in a way that could explain or justify the depravity of the Nazis' behavior. Like Job, the Jews suffered, and the magnitude of their suffering boggles the mind. Yet, unlike Job, whose suffering is ascribed to a contest between God and Ha-Satan (the Accuser), the Jews of Europe found themselves accosted by Hitler, who, to use Soloveitchik's terminology, may well be described as the man-Satan. The man-Satan, or Amalek,[8] is not a new enemy of the Jews. His story originates in Mosaic times and repeats itself time and time again. The mere presence of the Jew provokes the wrath of Amalek. It is completely absurd, unreasonable. But it is a reality, and Amalek's preoccupation with the Jew is all encompassing, as Soloveitchik notes.

> The hostility toward the Jew by Amalek, by man-Satan, is not directed exclusively against the religious Jew, who is conspicuous in his exoticism, who is different and unique. The hatred embraces religious as well as agnostic Jews, the nationalist Jew as well as the assimilationist Jew, the Jewish home adorned with a *mezuzah* and the home stripped of everything Jewish. The hatred of Amalek is

7. The Bible sets forth in many places the prophetic warnings given the Jews prior to the destruction of both the First and Second Temples. While the Jews of Germany had no such clear warnings prior to the onset of the Shoah, Hitler made no secret of his plans for the Jewish race were he ever to come to power. In 1925, Hitler published *Mein Kampf*, a book in which he claims that the Jews were conspiring to keep the Aryan master race from assuming its rightful position as rulers of the world. He further asserted that Jewish conspirators were to blame for the German defeat during World War I, and while not explicitly vowing revenge, Hitler's tone in the book is certainly threatening. From the perspective of 1945, *Mein Kampf* seemed to lay clear Hitler's intentions vis-à-vis the Jews of Europe, but in 1925, no one could be blamed for not taking him or his book seriously.

8. Amalek is, in Jewish tradition and rabbinic literature, the prototype of one who stands against God and belief in Him. Despite the humbling of Pharaoh and Egypt through the ten plagues and the destruction of Pharaoh's army at the Red Sea, the people of Amalek were quick to attack the Jews as they made their way out of Egypt. Amalek did not fear God and preyed upon the weak and helpless of His people (Deut 25:17–18). God would not forget this affront, and He commanded the Jewish people to do the same: "It will be, when the Lord your God grants you respite from all your enemies around [you] in the land which the Lord, your God, gives to you as an inheritance to possess, that you shall obliterate the remembrance of Amalek from beneath the heavens. You shall not forget!" (Deut 25:19–20).

commodious enough to encompass and embrace every Jew and every Jewish home.[9]

Again, our role is not to ask why. There may be no why, or if there is, it is certainly beyond us to comprehend it. We want to examine the response of the post-Shoah Jews, just as we did with the periods following the destruction of both the First and Second Temples. In those long-gone eras, the talmudic sages took on the role of spokespeople. They examined the deeds of the people; they searched for sins that might justify their suffering; and they proposed actions that the people could take to facilitate their repentance and return to God. Post-Shoah, many were too traumatized to speak or to share their experiences. And when they ultimately spoke, they generally did so for themselves. They told of their own experiences or of their own relationships with God. But there is one writer, one spokesperson, who, by virtue of his elegance, his consistency, and his perseverance, is now seen by many, myself included, as a representative for Hitler's victims, both living and deceased. In many respects, Elie Wiesel is a modern-day Job. He may not have the authority the talmudic sages had to speak for their respective generations, and admittedly, his views on the Shoah may not be reflective of those of each and every survivor. But in our time, in the sixty-plus years since the end of the Shoah, he has become a voice for many who cannot speak for themselves.

As we have previously noted, Wiesel, like Job before him, speaks of *dust and ashes*. Can Wiesel's use of this phrase—and others much stronger and harsher—and what appears to be God's reaction to them shed light on Job's utterance of *afar va-eifer*? The answer, I believe, is unquestionably yes.

Wiesel has used a variety of formats to express himself. His autobiography *Night* is perhaps best known, but Wiesel is also an essayist and a playwright, a relentless speaker who cries out against human suffering, be it of Ethiopians, Cambodians, Mesquite Indians, or Argentinian *desaparecidos*. As he noted in accepting the Nobel Peace Prize in 1986, "the list seems endless." We have already quoted *Night*. Let us consider other works that will put his *dust and ashes* references into perspective and will, in turn, do the same for Job.

In *Messengers of God*, Wiesel writes of a different contest involving man, God, and Ha-Satan. There is a midrash relating that God decided to prove to the Accuser that the first man, Adam, was the more intelligent of the two and thus worthy of his success. To do this, God summoned all the

9. Soloveitchik, *Days of Deliverance*, 17.

animals of the world to appear before Adam, who would then give them all names. One version of the midrash suggests that God cheated, that He asked the questions regarding each animal in such a way the Adam could not help but guess its correct name. Yet, argues Wiesel, there is a proof that God did not cheat and that Adam did not need Him to cheat. God asked Adam, what name will you give Me? Wiesel summarizes the conclusion to this midrash as follows:

> Adam rose to the challenge. He cast aside his humility and called God by His name. He understood intuitively that God Himself receives His name from man—illustrating the basic Jewish concept that while God is God and man is only His instrument, still God needs man to make Himself known, just as man needs God to acquire this knowledge.[10]

There is in Wiesel's worldview a notion that the bond between man and God is reciprocal and enduring. No matter who sees whom as dust and ashes, this bond remains. But it was sorely tested in the Shoah, and nothing in Wiesel's writings makes this clearer than his play *The Trial of God*. Set in the Ukrainian village of Shamgorod in the year 1649, this haunting play takes place in the aftermath of a pogrom. Only two Jews, Berish the innkeeper and his daughter Hannah, have survived the brutal Cossack raids. When three itinerant actors arrive in town to perform a Purim play, Berish demands that they stage a mock trial of God instead, indicting Him for His silence in the face of evil. Berish is described in the summary of the play as "a latter-day Job ready to take on the role of prosecutor." And how does this Jobian figure feel in the aftermath of his loss and suffering? How does he react when one of the players asks him, why not ask for God's mercy?

> BERISH. Because God is merciless, don't you know that? How long will you remain His blind slaves? I no longer rely on Him; I'd rather rely on the drunkenness of the priest. (*Sees the shock on their faces.*) What is it? You don't like the way I speak? How do you expect me to speak unless you want me to lie? God is God, and I am only an innkeeper. But He will not prevent me from letting my anger explode! He will not succeed in stifling my truth—and neither will you.
> MENDEL. What *is* your truth?
> BERISH. I don't know what it is, but I know that it is an angry truth! Yes, I am boiling with anger! Don't ask me why, you know

10. Wiesel, *Messengers of God*, 13.

why! If you don't, I do! But you do know why. You are in Shamgorod, you must know. To mention God's mercy in Shamgorod is an insult. Speak of His cruelty instead. You see what I mean?

MENDEL. I see. Continue.

BERISH. I want to understand why He is giving strength to the killers and nothing but tears and the shame of helplessness to the victims.

MENDEL. So—you don't understand. Neither do I. Is that enough reason to reject Him? Suppose you understood, would you accept?

BERISH. No, I would not.

MENDEL. Why not?

BERISH. Because I would refuse to understand—I would refuse to understand so as not to forgive Him.[11]

Berish's rant does not at all reflect the typical reading of Job's final response to God. Remember, we have examined a number of different translations of Job 42:6, and none resonate with the anger Berish does little to hide: "Therefore, I despise myself, and I repent in dust and ashes" (NRSV); "therefore I despise myself and repent in dust and ashes" (NIV); "therefore, I retract and repent in dust and ashes" (NASB).

Wiesel repudiates the traditional reading of the Jobian narrative even more forcefully in his essay on Job in *Messengers of God*. Calling Job "our contemporary," Wiesel, in reflecting on the dialogue between Job and God we have spent so much time considering, concludes:

At the end of his struggle, which Job recognized as being lost in advance—for how can man hope to defeat God?—Job discovered a novel method to persevere in his resistance: he pretended to abdicate before he even engaged in battle. Had he remained firm, had he discussed the divine arguments point by point, one would conclude that he had to concede defeat in the face of his interlocutor's rhetorical superiority. But he said yes to God, immediately. He did not hesitate or procrastinate, nor did he point out the slightest contradiction. Therefore we know that in spite or perhaps because of appearances, Job continued to interrogate God. By repenting sins he did not commit, by justifying a sorrow he did not deserve, he communicates to us that he did not believe in his own confessions; they were nothing but decoys. Job personified man's eternal

---

11. Wiesel, *Trial of God*, 42–43.

quest for justice and truth—he did not choose resignation. Thus
he did not suffer in vain.[12]

Wiesel does not see Job as one to portray himself as dust and ashes in
any meaningful sense. Perhaps he uttered the words as the traditionalists
have him doing, but, at least for Wiesel, in his heart Job knew to whom *afar
va-eifer* was really directed.

We are thus left to ponder what Wiesel's relationship with God is. In
Night he writes that the Shoah murdered his God. Through the character
of Berish, he seems to want little to do with God. And his characterization
of Job seems to reject the possibility of any open or truthful relationship
with God. Yet, if this is how Wiesel felt, he seems to have backed away from
these sentiments.

> And I became religious, even more so. The question to me was a
> double question. How come that I really became religious, more
> deeply than before? And the second one, how come I didn't lose
> my sanity? I never divorced God. I couldn't. I'm too Jewish. But I
> said to myself, "I do believe in God." But I have the right to protest
> against His ways. I have the right to be angry. And so, I do it a
> lot, very often, and I wouldn't change a word of my discourse to
> God, my appeals to God, against God. Because I came to a certain
> formulation saying a Jew or a man can be, can be religious or can
> come from a religious background, with God or against God, but
> not without God. So I cannot live without God.[13]

Wiesel concludes that he cannot live without God. Does he envision
Job living without God? No, he does not.

> Let us remember Job who, having lost everything—his children,
> his friends, his possessions and even his argument with God—
> still found the strength to begin again, to rebuild his life. Job was

12. Wiesel, *Messengers of God*, 234–35.

13. PBS, "Teaching Guide." Alan Dershowitz once reflected on Wiesel's ability to
maintain a relationship with God, saying, "There is a wonderful story about a great Chasidic master who was asked whether it is ever proper to act as if God did not exist. He
surprised his students by answering 'yes': it is not only proper, but mandatory, to act as if
there were no God when one is asked to help. Do not say 'God will help.' You must help.
Though Elie Wiesel is a deeply religious man—even when he argues with God or refuses
to forgive him—Wiesel acts as if there were no God when he is asked to help. I think I
understand why. He saw that God did not help his family and friends. He also saw that
human beings did not help, perhaps because they believed that God would help. Wiesel
knows that we cannot control God's actions, but we can control our own actions" (PBS,
"Teaching Guide").

determined not to repudiate the creation, however imperfect, that
God had entrusted to him. Job, our ancestor. Job, our contempo-
rary. His ordeal concerns all humanity. Did he ever lose his faith?
If so, he rediscovered it within his rebellion.[14]

If it is fair to view Wiesel as a representative and appropriate spokesperson for the post-Shoah generation—and I believe that it is—then it
seems clear from the works I have cited that this modern-day Job does not
or would not consider himself to be dust and ashes. I think it is more correct to say that Wiesel—and many of those who survived the Shoah—are
inclined to see God in that light. This is certainly not the humble or contrite
response traditionally associated with Job and with those who survived the
destruction of the Second Temple. We know that God ignored the pleas of
the latter or at the very least that their words and actions were not enough
to end their exile. Thus it is now time to consider how God responded to
the harsh words of Elie Wiesel and his contemporaries.

In the biblical period, God delivered His messages to the Jewish people via the words of the prophets. I want to suggest that in the post-Shoah
era, He seemingly has relied on human actions to speak for Him, and what
actions they have been!

On November 29, 1947, the United Nations General Assembly voted
33–13, with ten abstentions, in favor of a resolution recommending the
division of the British Mandate of Palestine into two states, one Jewish and
one Arab, with the Jerusalem-Bethlehem area under special international
protection, belonging to neither of the two states, and an accompanying
framework for overall economic union. Although a transitional period
under UN auspices was to begin with the adoption of the resolution and
was scheduled to last until the two states were established, US president
Harry Truman recognized the newly created Israel fifteen minutes after its
proclamation. As Truman would comment, "I had faith in Israel before it
was established, I have in it now. I believe it has a glorious future before
it—not just another sovereign nation, but as an embodiment of the great
ideals of our civilization."[15]

On May 14, 1948, the day before the expiration of the British Mandate, the Jewish Agency proclaimed independence, naming the country
Israel. The following day, the armies of five Arab countries—Egypt, Syria,

14. Wiesel, *Messengers of God*, 234–35.

15. Retrieved from http://thinkexist.com/quotation/i_had_faith_in_israel_before_
it_was_established-i/344150.html.

Jordan, Lebanon, and Iraq—attacked Israel. Saudi Arabia sent a military contingent operating under Egyptian command; Yemen declared war but did not take military action. After a year of fighting, a ceasefire was declared and temporary borders, known as the Green Line, were established. The newly established Jewish state had somehow survived this onslaught. Its new Prime Minister, David Ben-Gurion, summed up the feelings of the nation when he said, "Israel has created a new image of the Jew in the world—the image of a working and an intellectual people, of a people that can fight with heroism."[16]

More wars would follow: the Suez Campaign in 1956, the Six Day War in 1967, and the Yom Kippur War of 1973. Other conflicts, which the world chose not to see as wars but in which Jewish soldiers and civilians were nonetheless killed in defense of their reacquired homeland, included the War of Attrition from 1969 to 1970, the Lebanon Campaigns of 1978 and 1982, the Intifadas of 1987 and 2000, and the military operations in Gaza in 2009 and 2012. The Jewish state not only survived all these, it flourished, and it is hard not to see the hand of God behind most, if not all, of these events. Yitzhak Rabin, who was chief of staff of the Israel Defense Forces during the 1967 war, hinted at this in his postwar assessment: "Our airmen . . . struck the enemies' planes so accurately that no one in the world understands how it was done and people seek technological explanations or secret weapons; our armored troops . . . beat the enemy even when their equipment was inferior to his; our soldiers in all other branches . . . overcame our enemies everywhere, despite the latter's superior numbers and fortifications."[17]

True, Israel has its share of issues, both economic and political. Worse still, its people seem to have forgotten the lessons of history, for gratuitous hatred abounds, between the religious and secular, between the Left and the Right, and between Ashkenazi and Sephardi Jews. Yet, for all this, the Jewish nation continues to grow and thrive. Could it be that the people of Israel seem to intuitively understand what it means to partner with God and strive to complete creation? I think so, and perhaps so do others. As a business executive scouting digital-media companies in Israel wondered,

16. Retrieved from http://thinkexist.com/quotation/israel_has_created_a_new_image_of_the_jew_in_the/343786.html.

17. Sachar, *History of Israel*, 660.

"Why is all this happening in Israel? I've never seen so much chaos and so much innovation all in one tiny place."[18]

The facts and figures cited below are not meant to put a positive "spin" on the actions of the Jewish state or, worse still, to serve as a form of propaganda for it. Even its most vociferous supporters acknowledge its shortcomings and the political missteps it has made (and, according to some, continues to make). Rather, these facts should be seen as indicators of the extent to which a return to their homeland has enabled the Jewish people to fulfill their role as partners in the completion of God's creation.

Israel is the hundredth-smallest country in the world, and its seven million citizens make up about one one-thousandth of the world's population.[19] Yet, relative to its population, Israel is the largest immigrant-absorbing nation on earth, taking in 350 percent of its population in the past sixty years. Israel is the only country in history to have revived an unspoken language. Since the founding of the state, Israel has had more Nobel Prize winners per capita than any other country. It has more laureates in real numbers than China, Mexico, and Spain combined. Israel has the eighth-longest life expectancy (80.7 years), longer than the United Kingdom, the United States, and Germany.

Israel is the only country to enter the twenty-first century with a net gain in its number of trees, a fact made more remarkable given its arid climate. Over 90 percent of Israeli homes use solar energy for hot water, the highest percentage in the world, and Israeli companies are fabricating the largest solar-energy production facility in the world. Israel will be the first country to host a national electric-car network. Israel is ranked in the top five Cleantech countries[20] of the world and operates the world's largest desalinization plant.

Israel has had similar levels of success in the areas of science and technology. It leads the world in the number of scientists and technicians in the workforce, 63 percent more than the United States. It also has more physicians and engineers per capita than any other nation. Israel's scientific

18. Senor and Singer, *Start-Up Nation*, 16.

19. These facts and figures were retrieved from http://www.aish.com/jw/id/90725314.html. Similar facts and figures are cited by Senor and Singer, *Start-Up Nation*, 11–16.

20. Cleantech refers to a variety of technologies that seek to decrease environmental footprints and minimize pollution. These include recycling, renewable energy (wind power, solar power, biomass, hydropower, biofuels), information technology, green transportation, electric motors, and green chemistry.

research institutions are ranked third in the world, and its space sciences are ranked second. Israel produces the third-most scientific papers per capita, and the most in stem-cell science. More US patents are registered from Israel than from Russia, India, and China combined, and it leads the world in patents for medical equipment.

Israel is also a trend-setter in business. Israeli companies invented the drip irrigation system, discovered the world's most-used drug for multiple sclerosis, designed the Pentium NMX Chip technology and the Pentium 4 and Centrium microprocessors, and created Instant Messenger (ICQ). Israeli cows produce more milk per cow than any other cows in the world. Israel has the third-highest rate of entrepreneurship among women in the world. Israel has attracted the most venture-capital investment per capita in the world, thirty times more than Europe. Israel has more NASDAQ-listed companies than any country other than the United States—more than all of Europe, India, China, and Japan combined. In proportion to its population, Israel has the largest number of startup companies in the world. In absolute numbers, Israel has more startups than any country other than the United States.

As Rabbi Besdin once noted, "matching the Holocaust in power and mystery is the reconstitution of the State of Israel in May of 1948. Only a dogmatic agnostic would fail to see the transcendental overtones of this sudden transformation of Jewish dignity and hope."[21] And the accomplishments of the Jewish people since regaining sovereignty over their homeland is perhaps the apex of this dignity and hope.

The Jewish people in the post-Shoah era responded to their suffering in a way that their brethren did not following the fall of both the First and Second Temples. Like Job before them, the survivors of the Shoah found favor with God, and He restored them to their homeland. As Wiesel wrote, "I had ceased to be anything but ashes, yet I felt myself to be stronger than the Almighty, to whom my life had been tied for so long."[22] In this he was not alone. His generation experienced this same sensation and, also like Job, came to see God as dust and ashes. Though it be beyond our ability to comprehend, I believe this is what God had long desired from His people. Through this stance, through this usage of *afar va-eifer*, we were empowered, and this justified our return to our homeland. It was by no means a full restoration, just as the returning exiles from Babylonia un-

21. Besdin, "Holocaust," 138.
22. Wiesel, *Night*, 65.

derstood that their restoration was similarly lacking. But the restoration of the Jews' sovereignty over their historical homeland marks the beginning of a redemptive process for which Jews have been praying for nearly two thousand years.

CHAPTER 7

Abraham, Job, and the Need for Dust and Ashes

QUESTIONS AND ANSWERS. THAT'S what this has been about.

For the longest time, I assumed that mine was an unanswerable question. Thinkers and writers greater than me (at least those I've read) were seemingly as stumped as I was about why the Jewish people deserved to return to the land of Israel, their historic homeland, and reestablish their political and national sovereignty there. Then I stumbled upon what was, for me, an equally profound question, namely, whom was Job referring to with the phrase *dust and ashes*? Seeing this as answerable, at least in theory, I turned to text and history for answers. What else would a rabbi who is also a history teacher do?

Even the most casual reader of the Bible understands that it is a nuanced and layered text. Pick any of its books, and you will find commentaries, modern and classic alike, advancing differing approaches to translating and expounding its verses. The book of Job is no exception, and this is particularly true of the closing statement set forth in 42:6. As Samuel Balentine notes, "textual ambiguities make it clear . . . that whatever Job's last words may mean, they convey anything but a simple confession of sin."[1]

Yet, before we delve one last time into the intent of Job's final words, I would simply ask, Why? Why do we need the Jobian saga? Did not Abraham foreshadow Job when he challenged God's intended destruction of Sodom? Long before Job uttered the phrase we have been struggling with,

---

1. Quoted in van Voorst, "Dust and Ashes," 30.

Abraham likened himself to dust and ashes,[2] just as many commentators see Job doing later. Abraham addressed God with strong, almost inappropriate language, just as I contend Job does. "God forbid You do a thing such as this, to put to death the righteous with the wicked so that the righteous should be like the wicked. God forbid! Will the Judge of the entire earth not perform justice?"[3]

What, then, is the connection between these two biblical personalities? Abraham, like Job, was tested by God. Abraham, like Job, challenges the correctness and the justice of God's actions. In essence, Abraham partners with God in the events surrounding Sodom.[4] If so, Abraham has thus already set a precedent for challenging God's perceived injustice and for taking Him to task for doing so. Seen in this light, is not the book of Job redundant?

I think not, for I believe that Job resonates with us in a way that the Abraham of Sodom does not and cannot. First, were it not for Job, we might think that only an individual as great as Abraham has the right to challenge God and His actions.[5] More important, God, at the time of Sodom's destruction, was forging a special covenant with Abraham and his descendants, thereby creating a new nation to serve as a "light to the nations." As such, it was perhaps Abraham's right, as father of this new people, to challenge God concerning Sodom. In fact, a careful reading of the text shows that God seems to invite this challenge Himself by exclaiming, "Shall I conceal from Abraham what I am doing?" (Gen 18:17).

In sum, Job was a righteous individual before his trials began, but there seems to have been nothing in his righteousness that would give him special standing to confront God in the manner in which he did. Abraham may have preceded Job, but one could easily argue that he set no precedent for Job or for future generations to confront God in so direct and brazen a manner. Thus, without the Jobian narrative, none of us would dare question God as Job did.

2. Gen 18:27.

3. Gen 18:25.

4. See the Kli Yakar's commentary on the beginning of Parashat Vayeira (Gen 18:1—22:4), in which he contends that God invites Abraham to sit, as it were, in a *beit din* (rabbinic court) and judge Sodom. God remains silent and lets the contrast between Abraham's hospitality and Sodom's lack of it prove to Abraham the correctness of that city's impending destruction.

5. As great as Job might have been, he was no prophet, as was Abraham.

That is precisely the point of this study. In the end, it seems to me that Job does not humble himself before God. He stands up to God. Reading Job's closing words to mean that it is God Himself whom he refers to with the phrase *afar va-eifer* is not the only way to understand this verse. However, based on the context of Job's speech, the final outcome of his narrative and the weight of the rabbinic worldview of the Jewish people's history, it is certainly a plausible and, I believe, a very appropriate way to render it.

As we have seen, the strongest rationale for reading *dust and ashes* in this manner is the Shoah and its aftermath. What we have in the Shoah is the Jobian tragedy applied exponentially to an entire generation. Our task was not to explain or to justify the inexplicable and the unjustifiable. It was instead to show how the Jewish response to the Shoah—and God's reaction to that response—is fully consistent with our reading of *afar va-eifer*.

If we are correct in our contention that God's underlying intent when He breathed life into the first man was to create an empowered partner, then the Shoah can be viewed as the last of a series of seemingly incomprehensible events[6] intended to instill within the Jewish people a willingness to confront God about the unfathomable and arbitrary nature of their suffering. And if so, it was the Shoah that finally made the Jewish people say, "Enough! It is You, God, who is dust and ashes to us!"

Was it then God's initial intention to allow unmitigated cruelty and brutality to befall the Jewish people, all for their own benefit, all to mold them into the constructive force necessary to complete and perfect creation? I don't believe so. The rabbinic tradition places Job long before the destruction of the First Temple. His story was there, along with its lesson of how to become an empowered partner with God, if only we knew how to interpret *afar va-eifer*. God waited patiently, but as we have seen, the Jobian narrative was misread or, worse still, ignored. God thus decided to turn parable into reality, but He tempered this with mercy. How so? By combining two events, that is, this ignorance and inattentiveness to Job, which can only be swept away by a Jobian measure of suffering, and the sinful activities of the Jewish people, which also must be redressed via punishment and suffering. Seen in this light, the events surrounding the destruction of the First Temple had a twofold goal: punishment (to bring about repentance)

---

6. These include, in addition to the Shoah, events such as the destruction of both temples, the Crusades, the expulsion of the Jews from Spain, the blood libels of medieval Europe, the Chmielnicki pogroms in Poland in the 1600s, and czarist persecution of the Jews in the 1800s.

and suffering (to instill and inspire the empowerment of man needed for him to partner with God in the completion of creation).

Yet, as history shows, these events did not yield God's intended results. The Jewish people did not grasp the Jobian implications of the temple's destruction. Some suggest that they did not even repent. God then had no choice but to try again. Centuries later, He again brought suffering and destruction down upon the Jewish people. And once again, the Jewish people failed to get it. They repeated their sins, as the Talmud hints in describing the succeeding generations: "Ever since the [Second] Temple was destroyed, there is no day without a curse. And the curse of each day is greater than that of the preceding day."[7] Nonetheless, the Jews continued to misread Job and steadfastly saw themselves as dust and ashes. In doing so, they failed to elevate and transform themselves into the partners God wants and expects.

The Shoah was different, not because it was more brutal or more horrific but because the Jewish people finally understood that there is more than one way to read *afar va-eifer*. The Shoah was yet another inexplicable opportunity to show themselves worthy and empowered partners with God. They rose to the challenge. They no longer saw themselves as dust and ashes, which meant they were finally ready to work *with* God to restore Jewish sovereignty in Israel. And it was here that one profound question helped me answer another.

God returned the Jewish people to their land. It is up to them to rebuild it—and ultimately to build the Third Temple. There were some, such as Rabbi Yosef Yitzchok Schneersohn (known as the Freidicker Rebbe) and Rabbi Yoel Teitelbaum (known as the Satmar Rebbe), who thought that the suffering experienced by the Jews in the Shoah was so great that only by sending *Moshiach*, the Messiah, could God fully restore His people as He fully restored Job at the end of that narrative. But I think they had it wrong. To have sent *Moshiach* to do this alone—no matter how great their suffering—would have irreparably shattered the bonds of partnership between the Jewish people and their God. Why test them—as well as their readiness to be partners—only to deny them the chance to act as partners?

So, in our times, on whom does this burden, or better still, this responsibility, fall? Who has the right to so challenge God and partner with Him?

I have given this question much thought, and I'm not quite sure how to answer it. Perhaps the response Job gave only works on a national level.

7. *b. Avodah Zarah* 3b; *b. Berakhot* 32b; *b. Sotah* 49a and 48a.

Perhaps the individual needs to adhere to the traditional reading of the text, for to do otherwise leads to a slippery slope. Bad things do happen to people every day: divorces, bankruptcies, cancer, brain tumors, birth defects. These events do not happen simply because a person is sinful. Indeed, the talmudic sages have forcefully rejected the view of Rav Ami that "there is no death without transgression and no suffering without sin."[8] Yet, when these bad things happen, how can the individual really know what is justified and what is not? The risk, I believe, of the individual demanding answers or justifications is a rejection of God, something I have seen firsthand in friends who have experienced such suffering.

But the nation—perhaps this is different. Perhaps this is why Job was included in the biblical canon: to hint to us that although the individual cannot challenge God in such a way, cannot hurl accusations of being dust and ashes at Him, the Jewish people can. This is part and parcel of being God's chosen people, of being "a light unto the nations," of being His partner in the completion of creation.

We started our inquiry with Job himself and found an answer to my formerly unanswerable question in the aftermath of the Shoah. It is thus appropriate that we conclude by turning again to our modern Job, Elie Wiesel. In the introduction to *The Trial of God*, Robert Brown describes an experience Wiesel had in Auschwitz that at first glance leaves the reader dumbfounded. But to a people prepared to meet the challenge inherent in hurling the accusation of *afar va-eifer* at their God, it makes great sense. The response of Wiesel and the others present that night in the dust and ashes of the hell-on-earth called Auschwitz is one we should, I think, seek to emulate every day.

> One night the teacher took Wiesel back to his own barracks, and there, with the young boy as the only witness, three great Jewish scholars—masters of Talmud, *Halakha* and Jewish jurisprudence—put God on trial, creating in that eerie place, "a rabbinic court of law to indict the Almighty." The trial lasted several nights. Witnesses were heard; evidence was gathered; conclusions were drawn, all of which issued finally in a unanimous verdict: the Lord God Almighty, Creator of Heaven and Earth, was found *guilty* of crimes against creation and humankind. And then after what Wiesel describes as an "infinity of silence," the Talmudic scholar

8. *b. Shabbat* 55a–b.

looked at the sky and said, "It's time for the evening prayers," and the members of the tribunal recited *Maariv*, the evening service.[9]

9. Brown, "Introduction," vii.

Final Thoughts

THE THEOLOGIAN DAVID BLUMENTHAL notes that "in discourse with one another and before God, we must always speak the truth, as best we know it and can express it. Sometimes the truth is awesome; sometimes it is awful. But we owe it to one another, to the tradition and to God to speak the truth and to let the truth stand."[1] This is what I have tried to do in this work, to speak the truth as best I understand it. My understanding of *dust and ashes*, which gave me new insight into the book of Job and into the establishment of the state of Israel in 1948, seems both plausible and reasonable to me, even if it is not the only way to read the text.

In defining *theology*, Blumenthal writes further:

> Inter-pretation is the interaction of the personalities of God, the writers of the sacred texts, the readers and the teachers; hence inter-pretation is always plurivocal. The reader changes, the interpreter changes, God too responds to God's creatures. Time adds to the number of those who read and inter-pret. In the end, the text has more than one meaning, the reader reads on more than one level, and the teacher teaches more than one meaning. Text and life itself are multifaceted; inter-pretation is multidimensional. Plurivocity is normal; not hierarchy, not the single authoritative teaching. . . . To write theology is to resist the temptation to make authoritative declarations of doctrine, textual interpretation and religious practice. Rather, to do theology is to preserve the many-sidedness of R/reality.[2]

This work is very much a reflection of Blumenthal's approach to theological elucidation. I have made what I believe is a compelling case for my

1. Blumenthal, *Facing the Abusing God*, 237.
2. Ibid., 239.

interpretation of *dust and ashes* but never claimed that it is the only way to read the text. I do concede, as I have done throughout, that mine is a radical reading of the text. As such, there are sure to be those who will reject it out of hand and, by doing so, will also reject my understanding of the theological underpinnings of the reestablishment of the modern Jewish state. To do so, I think, would be a mistake.

When considering the book of Job, no matter one's views on Job's final speech, it is unarguable that Job is part of "a long tradition of the theology of protest."[3] From Abraham's arguing on behalf of Sodom[4] to Moses's defense of the Jewish people in the wilderness,[5] three basic themes of protest emerge from the biblical text: (i) questioning God over the issue of justice; (ii) appealing to God to act for the merit of the patriarchs, the covenant, or God's own name; and (iii) confession of guilt.[6] Yet another form of theological protest, that of national and personal lament, is evident from later sources such as Jeremiah and the Psalms.[7]

The rabbinic tradition built on these sources recognized the power and importance of explicit protest prayer (albeit offered by especially saintly rabbis and only under restricted circumstances).[8] The rabbis also recognized the value of protest in the midrashic literature. Ultimately, under the leadership of Rabbi Akiva, protest prayer fell from vogue and was replaced by the submissive-penitent form of prayer. However, "the tension between protest prayer and submissive prayer . . . could not be fully repressed, and protest prayer surfaced again in medieval religious poems, many of which were adopted into the liturgy."[9]

This theology of protest continued into more recent times, perhaps most powerfully and almost heretically in the protest-threat of the Kotzker rebbe:

> Send us our Messiah, for we have no more strength to suffer. Show
> me a sign, O God. Otherwise I rebel against You. If you do not

3. Ibid., 251.

4. Gen 18.

5. Exod 3; 32; Num 14.

6. Blumenthal, *Facing the Abusing God*, 251. Blumenthal primarily bases his analysis on Anson Laytner's *Arguing With God: A Jewish Tradition*. He also cites Muffs, *Love and Joy*, as a source for his arguments.

7. Blumenthal, *Facing the Abusing God*, 251.

8. Ibid., 252.

9. Ibid.

keep Your covenant, then neither will I keep the promise, and it
is all over: we are through with being Your Chosen People, Your
unique treasure.[10]

Based on these sources, as well as the Shoah and post-Shoah literature,
most notably the writings of Elie Wiesel, Blumenthal argues that challenge
is a proper religious affection. "Given our post-Holocaust setting and given
the continued insecurity of the Jewish people in the modern world, protest
is a religiously proper faith stance toward God."[11] In this respect, Blumenthal's theological position correlates precisely both with my analysis and
with my reading of *dust and ashes*. Yet, I am not willing to ignore those who
might dismiss my arguments because they consider my reading of *dust and
ashes* radical. I thus wish to step back and consider how the book of Job
and its implicit protest theology can help explain the reestablishment of the
state of Israel in 1948 even if I have misinterpreted *dust and ashes*.

Looking at the book of Job, it is clear that God found Job's closing
speech compelling enough to restore his health and wealth and to chastise
his three so-called friends.[12] This is true whether Job is calling himself or
calling God *dust and ashes*, and it is precisely this point that drives my
thoughts regarding the state of Israel.

The Jewish people in their long and often-tragic history have collectively faced three Joblike sets of circumstances.[13] The first involved the destruction of the First Temple. Unlike Job, the response of the Jewish people
to this enormous tragedy did not move God to restore them. Instead, He

10. Ibid. It is Blumenthal who describes this protest-threat as "audacious to the point
of being almost heretical."

11. Blumenthal, *Facing the Abusing* God, 253.

12. It is interesting to note that Blumenthal himself translates Job 42:6 as "'Therefore,
I am as nothing and I am remorseful, being [only] dust and ashes" (*Facing the Abusing
God*, 254. He seems here to agree with the views of Gordis (*Book of Job*) and Newsom
(*Book of Job*) that Job resolved his suffering by ultimately accepting his inferior status and
hence God's judgment. For Blumenthal, however, the more telling question is what became of the relationship between Job and God once Job "is reinstated in this world, better
off than he was." Did Job accept his second blessing without question? Did he resume
his pious life with reservation? See *Facing the Abusing God*, 255–57, for Blumenthal's
consideration of such questions.

13. I do not mean to suggest that other events, such as the expulsion from Spain or
the Crusades in medieval Europe, were not equally tragic or Jobian. They were, and they
certainly impacted the Jewish national psyche for centuries thereafter. Nonetheless, they
involved only part of the Jewish people (albeit a large portion). In contrast, the three
events I am about to discuss—the destruction of both temples and the Shoah—can be
said to have touched (directly or indirectly) the whole of the Jewish people.

waited seventy years before doing so, just as He said He would prior to the temple's destruction. We see this same pattern in the next Joblike event, namely, the destruction of the Second Temple. The rabbinic tradition holds that the Jewish people were extraordinarily contrite in the face of this disaster, humbling themselves and seemingly seeing themselves as little more than dust and ashes. Yet again, their response did not move God to act or to restore them to their homeland. It was only after the third and final Joblike event, the Shoah, that the Jewish people regained sovereignty over the land of Israel. Why is this? I maintain that their protests and challenges to God, equating Him with dust and ashes, set this generation apart from its predecessors and moved God to restore the people. This is how I read Job, and this is how I apply it to the events and circumstances of the 1940s.

And what if my reading of Job is wrong? What if the traditional reading of the text is the more plausible and more correct one? This does not change the fact that the Jewish people, like Job before them, responded to an overwhelmingly tragic set of circumstances in a manner God found compelling. Whether the post-Shoah generation of Jews saw themselves or God as dust and ashes is, in a sense, irrelevant. They, like Job, had their say, and God, I believe, responded.

In the end, this work tried to take on two enormously complex and seemingly irresolvable questions. The one ("who is dust and ashes?") helped me come to grips with the second ("why did the Jewish people merit the restoration of their homeland in 1948?"). Notwithstanding my linking the two, these are separate theological issues. As such, a rejection of my reading of *dust and ashes* should not negate or diminish my analysis of the Joblike response of the Jewish people in the aftermath of the Shoah and of God's reaction to that response.

Who Is Job?

READERS OF THE BOOK of Job tend to ask a very basic question: Who was he? Was he a Jew? A non-Jew? Was he a historical personage or simply the main character of a parable? Greatly diverse opinions exist concerning the origin of this book and the identity of Job.

One might have thought that questions regarding Job's existence had been put to rest by the prophet Ezekiel, who specifically mentions Job by name. "Then the word of the Lord came, saying: 'Son of man, if a land sins against Me by trespassing grievously, I shall stretch forth My hand upon it and break its staff of bread, and I shall send famine upon it and cut off from it [both] man and beast. Now should these three men be in its midst— Noah, Daniel, and Job—they would save themselves with their righteousness,' says the Lord God."[1]

Notwithstanding this reference, the rabbis of the Talmud posed the question of whether Job actually existed. Most took it for granted that he was very much a flesh-and-blood being, but there were many opinions about the epoch in which he lived and about his nationality. According to Bar Kappara, Job lived in the time of Abraham, whereas according to Abba bar Kahana he lived in the time of Jacob and married Jacob's daughter

1. Ezek 14:14. Rashi explains the reference to these three biblical personalities as follows: "Because each of these three saw three worlds: Noah saw the world built up, destroyed, and rebuilt; and Daniel, the Temple. Or himself: first a prince over all the princes, eventually cast into a lions' den, and [ultimately] restored to his greatness. Likewise, Job saw himself well-established, destroyed, and [again] well-established. Therefore, they were brought as a parallel to the generation of Jeconiah, which saw the Temple while it was built and while it was destroyed, and the [Temple's] second building."

Appendix A

Dinah.[2] R. Levi held that Job lived in the time of Jacob's sons, and, basing himself on Yossi bar Halafta, he maintained that Job was born when Jacob and his children entered Egypt. According to this view, Job died when the Israelites left Egypt, meaning that he lived 210 years.[3]

R. Levi's opinion is supported by a midrash stating that Satan came to accuse the Israelites living in Egypt of being idolaters.[4] In response, God set Satan against Job, and this became the source of Job's misfortunes. Additional support for R. Levi is found in *b. Sotah* 11a, where the text posits that Job was one of three advisors to the Pharaoh of the Exodus story. Specifically, the text maintains that Pharaoh consulted with three wise men of that generation—Job, Balaam and Jethro—prior to taking action against the Hebrews, who were increasingly multiplying.[5] What advice does Pharaoh receive? Balaam takes the most extreme position, urging Pharaoh to kill the Hebrews' newborn babies. Jethro opposes Balaam and advises Pharaoh not to harm the Hebrews. And Job? According to this text, he remains silent, and this silence, argue the talmudic sages, causes God to punish Job.[6] It should be mentioned that the narrative set forth in *b. Sotah* differs significantly from the version found in *Sefer ha-Yashar*.[7] There, Job is described as one of Pharaoh's eunuchs and counselors, and he is said to have advised Pharaoh to have every male child murdered.[8] Thereafter, Pharaoh had a dream that foretold the birth of a redeemer for the Hebrews, and he again consulted Job. This time Job answered evasively, saying: "Let the king do as he pleases."[9]

Others among the talmudic rabbis placed Job in more or less this same period. For instance, Levi ben Lahma believed that Job lived in the time of Moses (and in his view, the book of Job was written by Moses himself). Some declare that Job was the servant referred to in Exod 9:20: "He who feared the word of the Lord of Pharaoh's servants drove his servants and

---

2. *b. Bava Batra* 15a; compare additions in *Tg. Yer.* to Job 2:9.

3. Compare Rashi on Exod 2:40.

4. *Gen. Rab.* 1c.

5. See Exod 1:7–14

6. See also *b. Sanhedrin* 106a.

7. "Book of the Righteous," first published in 1811 in Vienna.

8. Exod 1:16: "And he said, 'When you deliver the Hebrew women, and you see on the birthstool, if it is a son, you shall put him to death, but if it is a daughter, she may live.'"

9. *Sefer ha-Yashar* 1c.

his livestock into the houses."[10] Raba, specifying the time more precisely, said Job lived in the time of the spies sent by Moses to explore the land of Canaan.[11] According to each of these rabbis, Job was a Gentile, albeit a pious Gentile, or one of the prophets of the Gentiles.[12]

The notion that Job lived during the time of Moses is not universally accepted. Some talmudic sages place Job variously in the reign of Saba, in that of the Chaldeans, and in that of Ahasuerus. R. Yochanan and R. Eleazar both declared that Job was one of those who returned to Israel from the Babylonian exile and that his *beit midrash* (house of study) was at Tiberias.[13] It is further stated in *b. Bava Batra* 15a that these sages necessarily considered Job an Israelite. Interestingly, R. Hananeel's version of *Bava Batra* read, "All the Tannaim and Amoraim, with the exception of the one who placed Job in the time of Yaakov, were of opinion that Job was an Israelite."[14]

There is, however, a minority opinion among the rabbis of the Talmud maintaining that Job never existed.[15] One of the later sages expressed this opinion in the presence of Shmuel bar Nachmani, holding that Job never existed and that the whole story was a fable.[16] Shimon ben Lakish seems to hold a similar view.[17] In his opinion, Job was the literary creation of a prophet and his story represents a parable of good and evil and of reward and punishment. The notion that the book of Job is merely a parable was subsequently adopted by many prominent sages. For example, though it is unclear which side of the debate he subscribes to, Gersonides suggested that the idea of Job as an allegory "is supported by the notion that it seems most improbable that there should be a discussion that would by chance encompass precisely all the possible opinions on providence."[18] Others, including Hai Gaon and Maimonides, are not so equivocal. According to

---

10. *Exod. Rab.* 12:3.

11. *b. Bava Batra* 15a.

12. *b. Bava Batra* 15b; *S. 'Olam Rab.* 21.

13. *b. Bava Batra* 15a.; *Gen. Rab.* 1c.

14. Compare also *Gen. Rab.* 1c.

15. *b. Bava Batra* 15a; *Gen. Rab.* 67.

16. *b. Bava Batra* 15a.

17. *b. Bava Batra* 15a; *Gen. Rab.* 57.

18. Eisen, *Book of Job*, 148. Rabbi Levi ben Gershom, better known in contemporary scholarship by his Latinized name Gersonides, is in Eisen's view one of the most remarkable intellectual talents in medieval Judaism. More pertinent to our study is the fact that Eisen believes Gersonides was inclined to see Job as a real person, not a literary construct, even though Gersonides never says so explicitly.

Maimonides, the parabolic nature of the book is reflected in the name of the country that is identified as Job's home, the land of Utz. Maimonides points out that the meaning of the word *utz* is both unclear and symbolic.[19] It can be a proper name, as is the case in Gen 22:21 ("Utz, his first born, and Buz his brother, and Kemuel, the father of Aram"). Alternatively, it can be read as an imperative form of the verb *utz*, which means "to reflect" or "to meditate." It is this second meaning that Maimonides prefers.[20] As Maimonides writes in *The Guide for the Perplexed*, "It is as if [scripture] said to you: meditate and reflect on this parable, grasp its meaning and see what the true opinion is."[21]

As interesting and compelling as all this debate may be, it is ultimately of secondary importance. Did Job exist or not? Was he a Jew or not? Was he a truly righteous man or not? These questions miss the point. The book of Job is an integral part of the Hebrew Bible, and when the rabbinic sages canonized the book, they were less concerned with the answers to these questions than with the message of the book itself. The lessons we learn from Job would be no less powerful if he were a literary creation rather than a real person and no less enduring were he a non-Jew rather than a Jew.

Joseph Grunblatt, reflecting on the continuing relevance of the book of Job in the face of the immense evil that characterized the twentieth century, understood this when he wrote,

> At times, the problem is brought into relief as the main feature of human concern, and no reference to its antiquity can assuage man's anger at his fate. Our post-Auschwitz generation is experiencing such a moment. It is not coincidental that interest in the Book of Job has increased considerably among students and seekers. The mid-twentieth century has witnessed what could Biblically be called *Hester panim* or what Buber called "the eclipse of God," unprecedented even in our calamitous history. . . . One Talmudic opinion ascribed to Moses authorship of the Book of Job (Bava Batra 14b). The very same Moses who saw God *be'aspaklariah*

19. The notion that Utz is a symbolic term is also found in the Talmud (*b. Bava Batra* 15a), but there it is related to the word *etz*, "tree." Maimonides's interpretation resonates with that of at least one prominent modern interpreter of Job, Norman Habel, who argues that *utz* could be a pun on the noun *etzah*, meaning "counsel" or "design," a word also related to the root *utz*, that is, "to reflect" or "to meditate" (Habel, *Book of Job*, 86). Habel points out that this association is appropriate because the notion of counsel or design is a common theme in Wisdom literature, of which Job is an example.

20. Eisen, *Book of Job*, 48.

21. Maimonides, *Guide for the Perplexed*, 486–87.

ha-me'irah (with the clarity of perception unequalled by any prophet), who heard the voice of God so precisely and with such definitude that he was able to receive the concrete word, "thou shalt" and "thou shalt not," the same Moses wrestles with the problem of evil through forty-two chapters only to have Job stand in submission before the *mysterium tremendum* that remonstrated with him from amidst the whirlwind.[22]

---

22. Grunblatt, "Great Estrangement," 66.

Destruction of the First Temple

A QUICK GOOGLE SEARCH of the words "the destruction of the First Temple" will yield a seemingly limitless number of hits. Yet, as with any internet search, it is hard to know which hits offer accurate or unbiased information and which do not. For this reason, I have included in this appendix a brief overview of the events surrounding the destruction of the First Temple. For those desiring a more detailed history, I recommend Binyamin Lau's *Jeremiah: The Fate of a Prophet*, published by Maggid Books.

The timeline for the destruction of the First Temple is relatively straightforward and begins more than 170 years before the temple's final destruction in 586 BCE. The unfolding disaster can be traced through the footsteps of various prophets, staring with Hosea (760–730 BCE), who prophesied during the northern kingdom's decline.[1] Remember that Nachmanides wrote that the events spelled out in the first *tochachah* did occur during the First Temple period: the worship of other gods, murder, theft, and sexual impropriety. And what the Torah foretold Hosea witnessed firsthand.[2] The prophet preached repentance, warning that exile would surely come if the people failed to heed his words. In the end, this is exactly what happened when Assyria captured Israel's capital at Samaria in 722 BCE.

The next prophet sent by God to warn the Jewish people of the coming consequences of their sinful ways was Isaiah (740–700 BCE). Isaiah lived

---

1. Upon the succession of King Solomon's son Rehoboam in approximately 930 BCE, the country split into two kingdoms: Israel (including the cities of Shechem and Samaria) in the north and Judah (containing Jerusalem) in the south.

2. See, for example, Hos 4:1–6.

in complicated and difficult times, when the political situation in Jerusalem was particularly volatile. His situation was further complicated by the fact that he prophesied through the reigns of several kings[3] and by the fact that he may have been a member of Jerusalem's ruling class: "His relations with the senior members of the royal house, as described in the Bible, and the fact that he had free access to the palace, together with the complex linguistic style of his prophecies, suggest that he belonged to the Jerusalem aristocracy."[4] This dual status meant that Isaiah could play an active role in events of the day and in some cases perhaps even guide them in a way that a "mere" prophet could not have.

God minced no words with Isaiah or the people: "In another sixty-five years, Ephraim shall be broken, no longer to be a people."[5] Isaiah therefore called on the people to put their faith in God and to seek his forgiveness. The king, at least, seemed to heed his call, and when Hezekiah initiated a number of religious reforms,[6] Isaiah felt hopeful: "Assuredly, thus said the Lord concerning the king of Assyria: 'He shall not enter this city; he shall not shoot an arrow at it, or advance upon it with a shield, or pile up a siege mound against us. He shall go back by the way he came, he shall not enter this city declares the Lord.'"[7] Despite his support for the king's reforms, Isaiah opposed Hezekiah's efforts to make military alliances with either Egypt or Babylon against Assyria. The prophet understood that, in the absence of true repentance by the people, neither would save the Jews from future foreign conquest. In fact, Isaiah specifically foretold that such alliances would turn out badly for king and country: "Behold a time shall come when everything in your palace and what your forefathers have stored up, shall be carried off to Babylonia; nothing shall remain, said the Lord."[8] Sadly, Isaiah was proven right.

Two other prophets previously discussed in this book, Ezekiel and Jeremiah, were particularly notable figures as the time of Judah's captivity and the destruction of the First Temple drew near, an event hastened by the

---

3. "The prophecies of Isaiah son of Amoz, who prophesied concerning Judah and Jerusalem in the reigns of Uzziah, Jotham, Ahaz and Hezekiah, kings of Judah" (Isa 1:1).

4. "Isaiah," *Jewish Virtual Library*, http://www.jewishvirtuallibrary.org/jsource/biography/Isaiah.html.

5. Isa 7:8.

6. 2 Kgs 18:1–6.

7. Isa 37:33–34.

8. Isa 39:6.

ascension of Nebuchadnezzar to the throne of Babylonia. Nebuchadnezzar became king upon the death of his father Nabopolassar in September 605 BCE, shortly after defeating the Egyptian armies under Pharaoh Neco at the famous battle of Carchemish. Soon after, Nebuchadnezzar turned his sights upon the Jewish kingdom. An initial invasion resulted in King Jehoiakim being made a vassal of the Babylonian king, but the Jewish king soon proved rebellious.[9]

In the face of this rebellion, Nebuchadnezzar returned with his armies. This second invasion came in 597 BCE and ended with the sacking of Jerusalem. King Jehoiachin was deported to Babylonia, and Zedekiah was placed on the throne in his stead.[10] Zedekiah was 21 years old when he became king, but his troubled reign lasted only eleven years, for "he did what was evil in the sight of the Lord."[11] The book of Chronicles describes the situation thus:

> He did not humble himself before Jeremiah the prophet, who spoke from the mouth of the Lord. He also rebelled against King Nebuchadnezzar, who had made him swear by God; he stiffened his neck and hardened his heart against turning to the Lord, the God of Israel. All the leading priests and the people likewise were exceedingly unfaithful, following all the abominations of the nations; and they polluted the house of the Lord which He had hallowed in Jerusalem. The Lord, the God of their fathers, sent persistently to them by his messengers, because He had compassion on his people and on his dwelling place; but they kept mocking the messengers of God, despising his words, and scoffing at his prophets, till the wrath of the Lord rose against his people, till there was no remedy. Therefore He brought up against them the king of the Chaldeans, who slew their young men with the sword in the house of their sanctuary, and had no compassion on young man or virgin, old man or aged; He gave them all into his hand.[12]

Ezekiel, a *kohen* (a member of the priestly tribe) who intended to enter the temple service at the age of 30, had an insider's understanding of the temple and its service. But he was taken captive in 597 BCE and appointed to care for the exiles in his company. Yet it is Jeremiah who is the more tragic of the two, for he was destined to remain in Jerusalem during

9. 2 Kgs 24:1.

10. 2 Kgs 24:15.

11. 2 Chr 36:12.

12. 2 Chr 36:12–17.

the final siege and destruction. It was he who specifically predicted both the destruction of Jerusalem and the subsequent seventy years of exile and captivity, a prophecy that figured prominently in our analysis. He also pronounced, as we have previously noted, judgment on Babylonia.

The actual destruction of Jerusalem (generally dated to 586 BCE) and severe suffering of its inhabitants are graphically described by Jeremiah in the book of Lamentations. A shorter and less graphic depiction of the final conflict appears in 2 Kings:

> On the ninth of the month, the famine became severe in the city, and the people of the land had no food. The city was broken into, and all the men of war [fled] at night by way of the gate between the two walls that were near the king's garden. And the army of the Chaldees pursued the king . . . and they seized the king and brought him up to the king of Babylonia, to Riblah, and called him to account. And they slaughtered Zedekiah's sons before his eyes, and they blinded Zedekiah's eyes, and he bound him with copper chains and brought him to Babylonia. And in the fifth month . . . Nebuzaradan, chief executioner, servant of the king of Babylonia, came to Jerusalem. And he burnt the house of the Lord and the king's palace, and all the houses of Jerusalem and all the houses of the dignitaries he burnt with fire. The entire army of the Chaldeans that was [with] the chief executioner demolished the walls of Jerusalem around. And Nebuzaradan the chief executioner exiled the remnant of the people who remained in the city, and the defectors who defected to the king of Babylonia, and the rest of the populace. . . . And the chief executioner took Seraiah the head priest and Zephaniah the priest of second rank, and the three keepers of the utensils. . . . And Nebuzaradan, the chief executioner, took them and brought them to the king of Babylonia, to Riblah. And the king of Babylonia struck them down and killed them in Riblah in the land of Hamat, and Yehudah went into exile off its land.[13]

---

13. 2 Kgs 25:3–25.

Destruction of the Second Temple

If the destruction of the First Temple was meant to be a clarion call to the Jewish people, to teach them the errors of their ways and to prompt a return to more proper service to God and His commandments, they either missed it or chose to ignore it, for in the end only a small percentage of the people opted to return to their homeland and rebuild the temple. Far worse, the Second Temple period was one characterized by serious internal strife and long periods of foreign domination.

The prophet Zechariah and his contemporary Haggai returned to Israel with the exiles from Babylonia, and it was they who inspired the building of the Second Temple. Better known as *shivat tzion* (the return to Zion), this period begins with the famous decree of Cyrus (the first king of the Persian Empire), issued at the close of the Jews' seventy years of exile.[1] The decree allowed the Jews to return to Jerusalem and rebuild the temple. Unfortunately, the effort to rebuild the temple in Jerusalem was initially thwarted by the complaints of the local population.[2] It was only some twenty years after their original return, when permission to build was

1. Ezra 1:1–3: "And in the first year of Cyrus, the king of Persia, at the completion of the word of the Lord from the mouth of Jeremiah, the Lord aroused the Spirit of Cyrus, the king of Persia, and he issued a proclamation throughout his kingdom, and also in writing, saying: 'So said Cyrus, the king of Persia, "All the kingdoms of the earth the Lord God of the heavens delivered to me, and He commanded me to build Him a House in Jerusalem, which is in Judea. Who is among you of all His people, may his God be with him, and he may ascend to Jerusalem, which is in Judea, and let him build the House of the Lord, God of Israel; He is the God Who is in Jerusalem."'"

2. Ezra 3:1—4:5.

finally granted by the Persian king Darius, in the second year of his reign, that construction began in earnest.

Zechariah commenced his ministry in the eighth month of the second year of the Persian king Darius Hystaspes.[3] The final two prophecies of Haggai were delivered on the twenty-fourth day of that same month and year. Thus, Zechariah's public ministry overlapped that of Haggai by approximately one month, and both men preached a message of hope, hope that the new temple would one day be greater than the first one, despite the obstacles placed in its way.

> The glory of this last House shall be greater than the first one, said the Lord of Hosts. And in this place I will grant peace, says the Lord of Hosts.[4]
>
> Sing and rejoice, O daughter of Zion, for, behold! I will come and dwell in your midst, says the Lord. And many nations shall join the Lord on that day, and they shall be My people; and I will dwell in your midst and you shall know that the Lord of Hosts sent me to you. And the Lord shall inherit Judah as His share in the Holy Land, and He shall again choose Jerusalem.[5]

Though Zechariah and Haggai are linked chronologically and thematically, it is difficult to determine what role Zechariah may have played in connection with the public ministry of Haggai. When they are mentioned together, Haggai's name is always first, suggesting either his leadership or his prophetic and canonical priority.[6] The most critical part of Haggai's appeal is arguably his addressing of the profound pessimism that had begun to envelop the people a few weeks after reconstruction began on the temple. They saw the new building as nothing compared to the glorious temple of Solomon. They therefore needed assurance that God was with them[7] and that eventually the glory of the Second Temple would exceed that of the First.[8] Significantly, within weeks (or even days), Zechariah followed this with a reminder of God's displeasure with their fathers' attitudes and ac-

---

3. Zech 1:1.

4. Zech 2:9.

5. Zech 2:14–16.

6. Ezra 5:1; 6:14.

7. Hag 2:4: "And now, be strong, Zerubbabel, says the Lord; and be strong, Joshua the son of Jehozadak the High Priest; and be strong, all the people of the land, says the Lord. And (for I am with you, says the Lord of Hosts) do."

8. Hag 2:7–9.

tions in the past. However, he also assured them that, if they turned to God, God would turn to them.[9] Both prophets contrast the past with the present and future, with Haggai stressing that the rebuilt temple would be a sign and source of God's blessing, whereas Zechariah emphasized the role of repentance and renewal in achieving that end. The two prophets complement each other's messages.

Notwithstanding the message of hope preached by these prophets, the Second Temple paled in comparison to the first, and the people quickly sensed this.[10]

> And many of the Kohanim and the Levi'im and the heads of the fathers' houses, old men who had seen the first Temple when its foundation was laid, [when they saw] this Temple with their eyes, were weeping with a loud voice, and many with a shout of joy to raise [their] voice. And the people did not recognize the voice of the shout of joy because of the voice of the people's weeping, for the people were shouting a great shout, and the voice was heard from afar.[11]

The people's weeping was justified. None of the ten miracles listed in *b. Avot* as occurring daily in the First Temple were manifest in the Second.[12]

9. Zech 1:2–3: "The Lord was wroth with your fathers, for they provoked Him. And you shall say to them: So said the Lord of Hosts, Return to Me, said the Lord of Hosts, and I will return to you, said the Lord of Hosts."

10. One might have thought that this diminishment was a natural outcome of the sins of the First Temple era, that is to say, that the temple, once sullied by sin, could never regain its former glory. However, as we learn in *b. Berakhot* 34b, "Rabbi Abahu said: Where *Ba'alei Teshuvah* stand, people who have never sinned cannot stand!" Rabbi Abahu understands the psychology of repentance to mean that the true *ba'al teshuvah* (literally, "master of return," but best understood as one who has "returned" to God) reaches a level of righteousness not matched by someone who has never "sinned." Admittedly, as Qohelet says, "There is no one so righteous in the world who does only good, but has never sinned" (Qoh 7:20). Nevertheless, Rabbi Abahu's dictum remains in force. In other words, those "sinners" who are able to muster up the spiritual resources to overcome their sins and return to God accomplish more than those who have rarely sinned. This suggests that had the people of the Second Temple era been worthy, had the repentance of the returnees from Babylonia been appropriately focused, their temple would have been every bit as great (if not greater) than its predecessor. Unfortunately, as we will see, they were not up to the task.

11. Ezra 3:12–13. Rashi explains that "those listeners did not recognize the voice of the shout of joy, because of the voice of the people's weeping, for the rejoicing people were shouting with a great shout, and the voice of weeping was heard farther and farther away."

12. See n. 218.

More important, the actions of the priestly class itself underscored the diminishment of the temple. According to the Talmud, during the First Temple period, which lasted about 410 years, there were only eighteen high priests. During the Second Temple period, which lasted 420 years, there were more than three hundred high priests. The Talmud reports that Yochanan was high priest for eighty years, Shimon for forty, and Yishmael ben Pabi for ten.[13] This means that in the remaining 290 years, there were at least three hundred priests, or approximately one every year or so. What accounts for this?

The Talmud relates that the Holy of Holies was forbidden ground except on Yom Kippur. On that one day only, the high priest was allowed to enter to perform special rites before God. If, however, he himself was not spiritually pure and was unable to focus, he would not be able to stand the intense encounter with God and would die on the spot. The Talmud recounts that during the Second Temple period a rope had to be tied to the high priest so that in the event he died in the Holy of Holies, his body could be pulled out.

The rabbinic perspective (as recorded in the Talmud) is both harsh and judgmental. In the rabbis' view, during most of the Second Temple period, the high priesthood was a corrupt institution, and this is why high priests frequently died or were replaced.[14] Nonetheless, people clamored for the job, and there was no lack of candidates for the position (which went to the highest bidder, not the most qualified). Thus, the question remains: Who would want the position, knowing that there was a great likelihood that he would die? One possible answer is that many of the candidates strongly believed that their incorrect temple service was actually the correct way to serve God.[15] This level of self-deception on the part of the unworthy candidates for the high priesthood had to have an impact on the masses, who for their part convinced themselves that they were faithful servants of God even though future events (namely, the destruction of the Second Temple) would show this to be untrue.

The political situation as portrayed in both biblical and rabbinic texts was not much better than the spiritual one. During the period of *shivat tzion*, many thousands of Jews did in fact return to Zion; however, many

---

13. *b. Yoma* 9a.

14. *b. Yoma* 9a.

15. See *b. Yoma* 19b for an account of the Sadducee high priest who died as a result of his improper actions while in the Holy of Holies.

thousands more remained in Babylonia. Despite these small numbers of returnees, Judea[16] was a nation within the confines of the Persian Empire whose leadership was entrusted to the high priest and a council of elders in Jerusalem. Even after its subsequent conquest by Alexander the Great of Greece in 332 BCE, the land remained a Jewish theocracy, first under Ptolemaic rule and then under the Syrian Seleucids. However, as the influence of the Seleucids grew over the years, Hellenistic influence crept into the land. This amalgam of Greek and early Eastern cultures grew dominant under the Seleucids, with Antiochus IV finally declaring Jerusalem a Greek *polis*, that is, Antiochia of Jerusalem. As a result, the Jews were prohibited from practicing their religion, and their temple was desecrated as part of an effort to impose Hellenistic culture and customs on the entire population. This led to open rebellion in 166 BCE. The revolt was first led by Mattathias of the priestly Hasmonean family and then by his son Judah (popularly known as "the Maccabee"). The Jews entered Jerusalem and purified the temple in 164 BCE, commemorated each year by the festival of Hanukkah.

Following further Hasmonean victories in 147 BCE, the Seleucids restored autonomy to Judea, and with the collapse of the Seleucid kingdom in 129 BCE, the Jews again achieved independence. Under the Hasmonean dynasty, which lasted about eighty years, the kingdom regained boundaries not far short of Solomon's realm. Political consolidation under Jewish rule was achieved, and Jewish life flourished once again, but this freedom from foreign influence and domination proved to be short-lived.

As has been the case throughout Jewish history, the difficulties that would arise were the result of a bitter rivalry between brothers, Hyrcanus and Aristobulus II. They came from distinguished lineage—their father, Alexander Jannaeus, was king and high priest. Their mother, Alexandra Salome, has been identified in rabbinical sources as the daughter of Rabbi Setach bar Yossei and the granddaughter of Rabbi Yossei bar Yochanan. After Alexander's death in 76 BCE, Salome succeeded her husband, thereby becoming the only Jewish regnant queen of Judea. She subsequently

---

16. The Bible recounts that after the death of King Solomon, Israel, sometimes referred to by scholars as the United Monarchy, split into two. Ten tribes followed Jeroboam, one of Solomon's officials, and formed the northern kingdom of Israel. The other two tribes remained loyal to Solomon's son, Rehoboam, who would rule the southern kingdom of Judah from Jerusalem. The territory of Judah roughly corresponds to the southern West Bank and northern Negev Desert of the modern state of Israel. In the Persian, Greek, and Roman periods, Judah is known as Judea.

installed her elder son Hyrcanus as high priest. Prior to her death in 67 BCE, she named Hyrcanus as successor to the kingship as well.

Hyrcanus's reign was both short and troubled. Three months into his reign, his younger brother Aristobulus II rebelled.[17] The armies of the two brothers clashed near Jericho, but many of Hyrcanus's soldiers went over to Aristobulus II, thereby giving the latter the victory. Hyrcanus fled to Jerusalem; but when the temple itself was captured by Aristobulus II, Hyrcanus surrendered. Hyrcanus renounced both the throne and the office of high priest but was allowed to enjoy the revenues of the latter office.

This arrangement did not last, however, as Hyrcanus feared that Aristobulus II was planning his death. Such fears were furthered by Hyrcanus's adviser Antipater the Idumean. According to Josephus, Antipater aimed at controlling Judea by putting the weak Hyrcanus back onto the throne.

As the Hasmoneans were allies of the Romans, both brothers appealed to Marcus Aemilius Scaurus (deputy of the Roman general Pompey). Each offered gifts and promises to win him, and in the end, Scaurus accepted a gift of four hundred talents of gold and decided in favor of Aristobulus. When Pompey arrived in Syria in 63 BCE, both brothers sent delegates to him seeking his aid in resolving their lingering dispute. Pompey, with an eye to the interests of the Roman Empire, would ultimately select the elder, weaker Hyrcanus over Aristobulus, deeming him a more reliable ally of Rome. While awaiting Pompey's decision, Aristobulus entrenched himself in the fortress of Alexandrium. When the Romans summoned their army, he surrendered and undertook to deliver Jerusalem over to them. However, many of his followers were unwilling to open the gates of the city, understanding that to do so would be to turn the city over to foreign control. In response, the Romans besieged and captured the city by force, badly damaging both city and temple. Aristobulus was taken to Rome, a prisoner, and Hyrcanus restored.

With this act, the Romans took control not just of Jerusalem but of the entire country as well. They maintained the pretense of a Jewish king, but in truth Hyrcanus had limited authority and was subject to the Roman governor of Damascus. Not surprisingly, the Jews were hostile to the new regime, and frequent insurrections followed. Mattathias Antigonus made a last attempt to restore the former glory of the Hasmonean dynasty, but his

---

17. A factor in their dispute was their differing religious outlooks. Hyrcanus shared his mother's religious views, that is, he was sympathetic to the Pharisees. In contrast, Aristobulus II agreed with his father's Sadducean stance.

defeat and death in 40 BCE brought Hasmonean rule to an end. The land was now just another province of the Roman Empire.

Unlike their counterparts during the First Temple period, the leaders of the Jewish people during the Second Temple era were left to decipher and interpret these events on their own, for "after the later prophets, Chaggai, Zechariah and Malachi had died, the prophetic spirit disappeared from the Jewish people."[18] Yet, the rabbinic leaders of the time did not need prophetic guidance to see that the end was growing near.

> Our Rabbis taught, During the forty years that Shimon HaTzaddik was Kohen Gadol the lot (for the scapegoat) always fell on the right side, from then on, sometimes on the right and sometimes on the left. The tongue of gold (a red string tied to the horns of the scapegoat) became white, from then on sometimes it became white and sometimes not. The western lamp remained lit (all night), from then on sometimes it remained lit and some times it went out. . . . Forty years before the destruction of the Temple the lot failed to come up on the right side, the tongue of gold did not become white, and the western light did not burn the whole night. The gates of the Hechel opened by themselves until Rabbi Yochanan ben Zakkai rebuked them.[19]

The Sages could not help but see that miracles that had previously been manifest now had stopped, and when they could no longer keep up a facade of law and order in the face of deteriorating circumstances, they removed themselves from their usual places of judgment.

> R. Kahana said, When R. Yishmael son of R. Yose fell sick, they [the Rabbis] sent [word] to him, Rabbi, Tell us the two or three things which you stated [formerly] on your father's authority. He sent back, thus did my father say: One hundred and eighty years before the destruction of the Temple the wicked State [that is, Rome] spread over Israel. Eighty years before the destruction of the Temple uncleanness was imposed in respect of the country of heathens and glassware. Forty years before the destruction of the Temple the Sanhedrin went into exile [that is, they forsook their locale in the Chamber of Hewn Stones in the Temple] and took its seat in the trade Halls.[20]

18. *b. Yoma* 9b.

19. *b. Yoma* 39a.

20. *b. Shabbat* 15a. See also *b. Avodah Zarah* 8b.

Perhaps the Sages had hoped that their actions would help the people understand the seriousness of the situation. They did not, and even though Rome's control of the land was complete, Jewish insurrection did not end with the defeat of Mattathias Antigonus. Rome would not and could not ignore these repeated challenges to its authority, and in 67 CE the empire's most experienced commander, Vespasian, was sent to Judea at the head of a massive force of four legions. Each legion had six thousand fighting men plus an equal number of auxiliaries, meaning that nearly fifty thousand Roman soldiers were sent to quash the Jewish rebels.[21]

The Romans were known for being brutal in warfare, but they surpassed themselves when it came to suppressing the revolt in Judea. Their aim was to send a message throughout the empire: any resistance against Rome would end in total devastation. To this end, Vespasian began his campaign in the north. Any city or town that resisted his advance was utterly destroyed, its population slaughtered or taken into slavery, the women raped, and property pillaged. Then, the surrounding area was denuded of trees and the fields strewn with salt to ensure that nothing would grow there again.

All during the summer and autumn of 67 CE, Vespasian marched through northern Israel suppressing Jewish resistance. Some cities, such as Tiberias, surrendered without a fight; others fought to the end. In this manner, the Romans had liquidated virtually all of the other pockets of resistance by the summer of 70 CE and had finally worked their way to Jerusalem. They surrounded the city and laid siege to it.

Before the Great Revolt began, Jerusalem had somewhere between 100,000 and 150,000 inhabitants, but with refugees from other places flocking in, the population had grown two to three times its normal size. It was concentrated in two enclaves—the Lower City, south of the Temple Mount,[22] and the Upper City, west of the Temple Mount, which was inhabited by the priests and the wealthy. The city was massively fortified. It also had huge storehouses of food and a good water supply. Its inhabitants assumed that Jerusalem could hold back the Romans for a long time.[23]

---

21. One of these four legions, the Tenth, was the most famous of its time and was commanded by Vespasian's own son, Titus.

22. This section of Jerusalem is today outside the city walls. It is called the City of David or Silwan in Arabic.

23. See *b. Gittin* 56a.

History shows that these assumptions proved false, for while the Romans were besieging the city, the Jews were waging a civil war behind its walls. Various Jewish factions occupied different parts of the city. Of these, the Sicarii and the Zealots, led by Yochanan of Gush Chalav, controlled the Temple Mount. An unlikely alliance of Sadducees and Pharisees made up the bulk of the moderate forces that ruled the rest of the city. When the moderates attempted to remove the extremists from the Temple Mount, Yochanan of Gush Chalav brought in non-Jewish mercenaries, the Idumeans, who slaughtered the moderate Jews. Compounding matters, the Zealots destroyed the great storehouses of food so that the people would have no choice but to fight or starve.

With the food storehouses destroyed, famine broke out in the city. One historian wrote that the severity of the famine was so great that "the bodies of the inhabitants were literally stacked like cordwood in the streets."[24] As had happened during the siege of the city prior to the destruction of the First Temple, mothers ate their children to preserve their own strength. People were desperate and tried to sneak outside the walls to forage for food. However, anyone caught by the Romans was immediately put to death via the standard Roman form of execution—crucifixion. Between the desperation of the people and the effectiveness of the Romans, the city was soon surrounded by thousands of crucified Jews. Indeed, the numbers grew so large that space was lacking for crosses and crosses were lacking for bodies.[25]

The final attack began just after Passover in the year 70 CE.[26] The city's defenders, weakened from hunger and from internal strife, should have been able to offer little challenge. Yet, it took two months of intense fighting before the Romans finally breached the outer city walls and reached the Temple Mount. The Roman historian Dio Cassius describes the events as follows:[27]

> Though a breach was made in the wall by means of engines, nevertheless the capture of the place did not immediately follow even then. On the contrary, the defenders killed great numbers

24. Stedman, *What's This World Coming To?*

25. Josephus, *War* 5.11.1.

26. In the interim, Vespasian was named Caesar and returned to Rome. He turned command of the legions over to his son Titus.

27. Unlike Josephus, who writes as an eyewitness to many of the events he records, Dio Cassius lived later and merely repeated what he had read in official Roman records.

[of Romans] who tried to crowd through the opening and they also set fire to some of the buildings nearby, hoping thus to check the further progress of the Romans. Nevertheless, the soldiers, because of their superstition, did not immediately rush in but at last, under compulsion from Titus, they made their way inside. Then the Jews defended themselves much more vigorously than before, as if they had discovered a piece of rare good fortune in being able to fight near the Temple and fall in its defense.[28]

Slaughter ensued, with the Romans taking the city house by house. Despite the determined resistance of the Jewish defenders, Titus and his legions slowly worked their way to the Temple Mount. Once there, Titus ordered the Second Temple razed to the ground. Dio Cassius describes the scene:

The populace was stationed below in the court and the elders on the steps and the priests in the Sanctuary itself. And though they were but a handful fighting against a far superior force, they were not conquered until part of the Temple was set on fire. Then they met their death willingly, some throwing themselves on the swords of the Romans, some slaying one another, others taking their own lives and still others leaping into the flames. And it seemed to everybody and especially to them that so far from being destruction, it was victory and salvation and happiness to them that they perished along with the Temple.[29]

All of the neighboring countryside had been denuded of whatever trees remained from the siege to create the giant bonfire to burn the buildings of the temple to the ground. The intense heat from the fire caused the moisture in the limestone to expand, and it exploded like popcorn, producing a chain reaction of destruction. In a day's time, the Second Temple was nothing but rubble. Josephus was there to witness the destruction:

These Romans put the Jews to flight, and proceeded as far as the holy house [the Temple] itself. At which time one of the soldiers, without staying for any orders, and without any concern or dread upon him at so great an undertaking, and being hurried on by a certain divine fury, snatched somewhat out of the materials that were on fire, and being lifted up by another soldier, he set fire to a golden window, through which there was a passage to the rooms

28. Cassius Dio, *Roman History*, 66.6; text from http://penelope.uchicago.edu/ Thayer/E/Roman/Texts/Cassius_Dio/65*.html.

29. Ibid.

that were round about the holy house, on the north side of it. As the flames went upward, the Jews made a great clamor, such as so mighty an affliction required, and ran together to prevent it; and now they spared not their lives any longer, nor suffered anything to restrain their force, since that holy house was perishing. . . . Thus it was the holy house burnt down. . . . Nor can one imagine any thing greater or more terrible than this noise; for there was at once a shout of the Roman Legions, who were marching all together, and a sad clamor of the seditious, who were now surrounded with fire and sword. . . . The people under a great consternation, made sad moans at the calamity they were under. . . . Yet was the misery itself more terrible than this disorder; for one would have thought that the hill itself, on which the Temple stood, was seething hot, as full of fire on every part of it.[30]

It was a terrible disaster for the Jews. Hundreds of thousands of people died; many more were enslaved.[31] There were so many Jews flooding the slave market after the Great Revolt that it was said that one could buy a Jewish slave for less than the price of a horse. Congratulating themselves on asserting their might against the defiant Jews, the Romans minted coins depicting a weeping woman and proclaiming *Iudea capta,* "Judea Captured." Josephus tried to sum up the horrendous outcome, but even he seems to concede that his eyewitness report fails to capture the magnitude of the suffering the Jews:

No destruction ever wrought by God or man approached the wholesale carnage of this war. Every man who showed himself was either killed or captured by the Romans, and then those in the sewers were ferreted out, the ground was torn up and all who were trapped were killed. There too were found the bodies of more than 2,000, some killed by their own hand, some by one another's, but most by starvation. So foul a stench of human flesh greeted those who charged in that many turned back at once. Others were so

30. Josephus, *War* 6.5.1. Josephus would have us believe that Titus tried to prevent the destruction of the temple, but the accuracy of such a claim is greatly in doubt. Josephus, who was at this point working for the Romans and became an adopted member of the family of Vespasian and Titus, certainly tried to paint the Romans in the best light possible.

31. Josephus estimates that more than one million Jews perished during the revolt, which culminated with the destruction of the Second Temple. Zeitlin, *Rise and Fall,* 410, writes that the Romans showed no mercy to the vanquished and that their slaughter of the inhabitants of Jerusalem was so immense that Herod begged the Roman military leaders to call a halt to it.

avaricious that they pushed on, climbing over the piles of corpses; for many valuables were found in the passages and all scruples were silenced by the prospect of gain. . . . But neither its long history, nor its vast wealth, nor its people dispersed through the whole world, nor the unparalleled renown of its worship sufficed to avert its ruin. So ended the siege of Jerusalem.[32]

32. Josephus, *War*, 6.10.1.

A Brief History of Zionism

FORMALLY DEFINED, ZIONISM IS a form of nationalism of Jews and Jewish culture that supports a Jewish nation-state in the territory defined as the land of Israel. The first wave of Jews to return to their historic homeland, then called Palestine, took place between 1882 and 1903. Commonly referred to as the First Aliyah, approximately 35,000 Jews immigrated to the southwestern area of Syria, then a province of the Ottoman Empire. The majority, belonging to the Hovevei Zion and Bilu movements (two organizations considered to be forerunners and foundation-builders of modern Zionism), came from the Russian Empire, with a smaller number arriving from Yemen.

An equally significant and crystallizing event took place in the year 1894, not in Israel but in France. At the center of it all was a Jew, Captain Alfred Dreyfus, who was accused and convicted of treason. His alleged crime: communicating French military secrets to the Germans during the Franco-Prussian War of 1870. Dreyfus was sent to the penal colony at Devil's Island in French Guiana, where he spent almost five years. The Dreyfus Affair, as it came to be known, created a political scandal that divided France.

The scourge of anti-Semitism was manifest during the trial, and shouts of "death to the Jews" could be heard in many French towns. A young Austrian journalist named Theodor Herzl was covering the trial, and though he was a thoroughly assimilated Jew, educated in the spirit of the German Jewish enlightenment, the events he witnessed in France had a profound impact on him.

In the aftermath of the Dreyfus Affair, Herzl came to the realization that anti-Semitism was an ever-present factor in human society and could not be overcome by assimilation of individual Jews in their respective countries. For Herzl, the essence of the Jewish problem was not individual but national, and he put forward his ideas in *Der Judenstaat* (The Jewish State), published in 1896. In this work, Herzl declared that the Jews could gain acceptance in the world only if they ceased being a national anomaly. The Jews are one people, he argued, and their plight could be transformed into a positive force by the establishment of a Jewish state with the consent of the great powers. He saw the Jewish question as an international political question to be dealt with in the arena of international politics.

Herzl proposed a practical program for collecting funds from Jews around the world by a company, to be owned by stockholders, that would work toward the practical realization of this goal. (This organization, when it was eventually formed, was called the Zionist Organization.) He saw the future state as a model social state, basing his ideas on the European model of a modern, enlightened society. It would be neutral, peace-seeking, and of a secular nature.

In a later work, the Zionist novel *Altneuland* (Old New Land, 1902), Herzl pictured the future Jewish state as a socialist utopia. He envisioned a new society that was to rise in the land of Israel on a cooperative basis, utilizing science and technology in the development of the land.

He included detailed ideas about how he saw the future state's political structure, immigration, fundraising, diplomatic relations, social laws, and relations between religion and the state. In *Altneuland*, the Jewish state was envisioned as a pluralist, advanced society, a "light unto the nations." This book had a significant impact on the Jews of the time and became a symbol of the Zionist vision for the land of Israel.

Under Herzl's leadership, Jews from around the world gathered in 1897 in Basel, Switzerland. Herzl convened this First Zionist Congress (as it was called) as a symbolic parliament. It unquestionably generated great enthusiasm throughout the Jewish world, but sharp criticisms of Zionism, too, began to appear, claiming that Zionism could not hope to resolve the Jewish problem and would only serve to harm the status of Jewish laborers and sabotage recognition of Jewish laborers as an independent class. In fact, this first congress, which was originally scheduled to take place in Munich, was moved to Basel in the face of vocal opposition by the local leadership of both the Orthodox and Reform communities.

On the second day of deliberations (August 30, 1897), members of the congress passed a declaration stating that "Zionism seeks to establish a home for the Jewish people in Palestine secured under public law." This gave clear expression to Herzl's political Zionist vision, in contrast to the settlement-oriented activities of the more loosely organized Hovevei Zion, the organization that had helped bring the first Jewish settlers to the land in the early 1880s. To satisfy the request of numerous delegates who sought the inclusion of the phrase "by international law," a compromise formula proposed by Herzl was eventually adopted.

The program, which came to be known as the Basel Program, set out the goals of the Zionist movement. It was adopted in the following terms:

> Zionism aims at establishing for the Jewish people a publicly and legally assured home in Palestine. For the attainment of this purpose, the Congress considers the following means serviceable:
>
> 1. The promotion of the settlement of Jewish agriculturists, artisans, and tradesmen in Palestine.
>
> 2. The federation of all Jews into local or general groups, according to the laws of the various countries.
>
> 3. The strengthening of the Jewish feeling and consciousness.
>
> 4. Preparatory steps for the attainment of those governmental grants which are necessary to the achievement of the Zionist purpose.

Subsequent congresses founded various institutions for the promotion of this program, notably a people's bank known as the Jewish Colonial Trust, which was the financial arm of political Zionism. Its establishment was suggested at the First Zionist Congress in 1897; the first definite steps toward its institution were taken at the Second Zionist Congress in Cologne, Germany, in May 1898. The Fifth Zionist Congress saw the founding of the Jewish National Fund, for the purchase of land in Israel. The Zionist Commission and its subsidiary societies were founded somewhat later, for the study and improvement of the social and economic condition of the Jews within the land of Israel.

The Zionist Congress met every year between 1897 and 1901 in an effort to advance the Basel Program. It was during this time that Herzl turned to Great Britain and met with Joseph Chamberlain, the British colonial secretary, and others. The British agreed, in principle, to Jewish settlement in East Africa, "on conditions which will enable members to observe their national customs."[1] At the Sixth Zionist Congress, held in Basel in August 1903, Herzl proposed the British Uganda Program as a temporary refuge for Jews in Russia in immediate danger as a result of the pogroms then taking place. (Pogroms against the Jews were a common occurrence in the Russian Empire, and the most infamous of these included the Odessa pogroms of 1881 and 1886, the Warsaw pogrom of 1881, and the Kishinev pogrom of 1903.) By a vote of 295–178, it was decided to send an expedition ("investigatory commission") to examine the territory proposed.

Though Herzl made it clear that this program would not affect the ultimate aim of Zionism, namely, a Jewish entity in the land of Israel, the proposal aroused a storm of protest at the congress and nearly led to a split in the Zionist movement. The Jewish Territorialist Organization (ITO) was formed as a result of the unification of various groups who had supported Herzl's Uganda proposal. In the end, the Uganda Plan put forward by Herzl was rejected in 1905 at the Seventh Zionist Congress, a decision Herzl did not live to see. To the end, finding a solution to the Jewish problem dominated Herzl's thoughts. A day before his death on July 3, 1904, Herzl told the Reverend William H. Hechler: "Greet Palestine for me. I gave my heart's blood for my people."[2]

The Jewish people, especially those already living in Palestine, mourned Herzl's passing, but even the passing of this great visionary did little to slow the momentum of the Zionist enterprise. Between 1904 and 1914, approximately forty thousand Jews emigrated in the Second Aliyah, spurred to leave Russia in the face of pogroms and outbreaks of anti-Semitism in that country. These immigrants were greatly influenced by socialist ideals, and they sought to put their ideals into practice by establishing the first kibbutz, Degania, in 1909. They also formed self-defense organizations, such as Hashomer, to counter increasing Arab hostility and to help Jews to protect their communities from Arab bandits.

It was during this period, in 1906, that David Ben-Gurion arrived in Israel. No story of the founding of the modern Jewish state would be complete without Ben-Gurion, but his list of accomplishments is too extensive for any overview of the history of Zionism. In brief, Ben-Gurion's passion

1. "Zionist Congress," *Jewish Virtual Library*, http://www.jewishvirtuallibrary.org/jsource/Zionism/Uganda.html.

2. "Theodor Herzl: Founder of Modern Zionism," *Spokeo*, http://www.spokeo.com/Theodor+Herzl+1.

for Zionism began early in life and drove him to key leadership positions, including executive head of the World Zionist Organization, head of the Jewish Agency, president of the Jewish Agency Executive, and, ultimately, de facto leader of the Jewish community in Palestine during its struggle for an independent Jewish state. It was Ben-Gurion who, on May 14, 1948, formally proclaimed the establishment of the State of Israel, and he was the first to sign the Israeli Declaration of Independence, a document that he helped write. Not without justification is he frequently referred to as "Israel's founding father."

When Israel's War of Independence ended in 1949, Ben-Gurion was selected as the fledgling nation's first Prime Minister, a post he held until 1963 (except for a period of nearly two years between 1954 and 1955 when he served as the country's defense minister). In this capacity, he faced many challenges, not the least of which were building state institutions necessary to run the country and launching various national projects (such as the construction of the National Water Carrier) aimed at fostering its economic development. All the while he was also overseeing the absorption of vast numbers of Jews from around the world, a task that included Operation Magic Carpet, the airlift of Jews from various Arab countries. This influx of new citizens in turn required numerous rural development projects and the establishment of new towns and cities.

Posthumously, Ben-Gurion was named one of *Time*'s 100 Most Important People of the Twentieth Century.

In 1917, Chaim Weizmann became president of the British Zionist Federation and was soon able to convince the British government to issue the Balfour Declaration of November 2, 1917. In brief, this declaration encompassed a letter from the United Kingdom's foreign secretary, Arthur James Balfour, to the Zionist Federation of Great Britain and Ireland. It read as follows: "His Majesty's government view with favour the establishment in Palestine of a national home for the Jewish people, and will use their best endeavours to facilitate the achievement of this object, it being clearly understood that nothing shall be done which may prejudice the civil and religious rights of existing non-Jewish communities in Palestine, or the rights and political status enjoyed by Jews in any other country."[3]

The Balfour Declaration engendered much hope and optimism among the Jews. Indeed, from 1919 to 1923 approximately forty thousand

3. "Balfour Declaration," http://unispal.un.org/UNISPAL.NSF/0/ E210CA73E38D9E1D052565FA00705C61.

Jews immigrated to Palestine as part of the Third Aliyah. This influx came mainly from the Russian Empire in response to a number of factors, in addition to the Balfour Declaration, including the end of World War I, the British conquest of Palestine, and the establishment of the Palestinian Mandate by the League of Nations.[4] Many of these immigrants were pioneers, known as *halutzim*, trained in agriculture and capable of establishing self-sustaining economies. In spite of immigration quotas established by the British administration, the population of Jews reached ninety thousand by the end of this period.

The 1920s saw a number of important figures in the Zionist movement arrive on the scene. For instance, in 1920, Chaim Weizmann, who had demonstrated his skills and political savvy with the Balfour Declaration, became president of the World Zionist Organization. He would later serve as the first president of the state of Israel. In 1921, another of the nation's founders, Golda Meir, arrived in Israel. Meir earned her fame in prestate Israel when, in 1948, she traveled to the United States and managed to raise $50 million, which was used to purchase arms for Israel's new army. Ben-Gurion wrote that Meir's role as the "Jewish woman who got the money which made the state possible" would go down one day in the history books.[5] Of equal note, four days before the official establishment of the state in 1948, Meir traveled to Amman disguised as an Arab woman for a secret meeting with King Abdullah of Transjordan, at which she urged the king not to join other Arab countries in attacking the Jews. Abdullah asked her not to hurry to proclaim a state. Meir replied: "We've been waiting for 2,000 years. Is that hurrying?"[6] Like Ben-Gurion, Meir would also serve as prime minister of Israel and in the process become the world's third woman to serve as prime minister of a democratically elected government.

The 1920s are also known in Zionist history for the Fourth Aliyah, during which 82,000 Jews fled the anti-Semitism of Poland and Hungary to build new lives as part of the Jewish settlement in Palestine. These newest

---

4. The civil administration was formalized with the League of Nations' consent in 1923 under the British Mandate for Palestine, which covered two administrative areas. The land west of the Jordan River, known as Palestine, was under direct British administration until 1948, and the land east of the Jordan was a semiautonomous region known as Transjordan, under the rule of the Hashemite family, and gained independence in 1946.

5. "Golda Meir," *Spokeo*, http://www.spokeo.com/Golda+Meir+1.

6. "Who Is Golda Meir?," *WiseGeek*, http://www.wisegeek.com/who-is-golda-meir. htm#didyouknowout.

immigrants to Palestine included many middle-class families who had the means and the wherewithal to establish small businesses and light industry.

This decade is also remembered for a sharp escalation in violence between Jewish immigrants to Palestine and Arab population who had been living there for hundreds of years under Turkish and then British rule. The most infamous of these incidents occurred in 1929. First came the Palestine Riots, also known as the Western Wall Uprising. This refers to a series of demonstrations and riots in late August 1929, when a long-running dispute between Muslims and Jews over access to the Western Wall in Jerusalem escalated into violence. During the week of riots, 116 Arabs and 133 Jews were killed and 232 Arabs and 198 Jews were injured and treated in hospitals. According to the official report, "many of the Arab casualties and possibly some of the Jewish casualties were caused by rifle fire by the police or military forces."[7] Then came the Hebron Massacre, in which sixty-eight Jews were murdered and another fifty-eight were wounded. This massacre effectively ended more than two thousand years of continuous Jewish presence in the city of Hebron.

As was the case throughout the early years of the Zionist movement, apparent setbacks only served to strengthen the determination of the Jews to reestablish a homeland for themselves in Israel. This was certainly the case during the years 1929–1939, when the Fifth Aliyah took place. With the rise of Nazism in Germany, a new wave of 250,000 Jewish immigrants arrived in Palestine. The majority of these, 174,000, arrived between 1933 and 1936, after which increasing restrictions on immigration by the British made immigration clandestine and illegal. The Fifth Aliyah, like those before it, was largely made up of immigrants from Eastern Europe but also included professionals, doctors, lawyers, and professors from Germany.

The Arab population of Palestine was not passive in the face of these waves of Jewish immigration. Violence became an everyday event, and in 1936 Arab riots in Jerusalem led to a virtually Jew-free "Muslim Quarter." (To this day, it is possible to see indications of the former Jewish population in Jerusalem's Muslim Quarter, most notably, the carved spaces in the stone doorframes in which, prior to the 1936 riots, Jewish residents had placed *mezuzot*.)

Illegal immigration became increasingly common from 1933 to 1948. During this time, the British government placed quotas on Jewish immigration to Palestine, and following the rise of Nazism in Germany, illegal

7. "1929 Palestine Riots," http://shelf3d.com/i/1929%20Palestine%20riots.

immigration to Palestine grew. This illegal immigration was known as Aliyah Bet ("secondary immigration"), or Ha'apalah, and conditions at the time tested the bravery and ingenuity of the immigrants who were forced to travel mainly by sea and to a lesser extent overland through Iraq and Syria. During World War II and until 1948, Aliyah Bet was the main form of Jewish immigration to Palestine.

Aliyah Bet brought with it another important prewar leader and future prime minister of Israel, Menachem Begin, who arrived in Israel in 1942. During the prestate era, Begin was the leader of the Zionist militant group Irgun, a Revisionist group that broke away from the larger Jewish paramilitary organization Haganah. After the establishment of the state, he was elected to the first Knesset, as head of Herut, the party he founded. For decades, Herut was on the fringe of Israeli politics, standing in opposition to the Mapai-led government and Israeli establishment.[8] This made his 1977 electoral victory and assumption of the office of prime minister all the more remarkable.

Begin's most significant achievement as prime minister was the signing of a peace treaty with Egypt in 1979, for which he and Anwar Sadat shared the Nobel Peace Prize.

After World War II, the establishment of the state was driven by the United Nations' partition plan for Palestine, which was adopted in November 1947. This plan set forth the details of an economic union that was intended, after the termination of the British Mandate, to facilitate the creation of independent Arab and Jewish states. The plan also included a detailed description of the proposed boundaries for each state and called for the protection of religious and minority rights and for a special international regime for the city of Jerusalem.

According to this plan, the new Arab and Jewish states were to come into existence two months after the withdrawal of British troops from Palestine, but no later than October 1, 1948. Though the borders of the proposed Jewish state were not what Ben-Gurion and the other leaders of the Jews of Palestine had hoped for, the Jewish Agency accepted the parameters of the partition plan. However, the Arab community of Palestine, as well as the governments of the neighboring Arab countries, rejected it outright. Immediately after the plan's adoption by a resolution of the General

---

8. Mapai (Mifleget Poalei Eretz Israel, or Land of Israel Worker's Party) was established in 1930 as a Zionist Socialist party and was the dominant political party in the prestate and early poststate years.

Assembly of the United Nations, hostilities between Arabs and Jews broke out throughout Palestine. As a result, the partition plan was never formally implemented.

On Friday, May 14, 1948, in a ceremony in the Tel Aviv Museum (today known as Independence Hall) beginning promptly at 4:00 p.m. (a time chosen so as not to breach the Jewish Sabbath), David Ben-Gurion declared the independence of the fledgling Jewish state. His remarks and his reading of Israel's Declaration of Independence were broadcast live as the first transmission of the new radio station Kol Yisrael.[9]

Ben-Gurion opened the ceremony by banging his gavel on the table, prompting a spontaneous rendition of "Hatikvah," soon to be Israel's national anthem, from the 250 guests. On the wall behind the podium hung a picture of Theodor Herzl, the founder of modern Zionism, and a flag which would later become the official flag of Israel.

After telling the audience "I shall now read to you the scroll of the Establishment of the State, which has passed its first reading by the National Council," Ben-Gurion proceeded to read out the declaration, ending with the words "Let us accept the Foundation Scroll of the Jewish State by rising" and calling on Rabbi Fishman to recite the Shehecheyanu: "Blessed are You, Lord our God, Ruler of the Universe who has granted us life, sustained us and enabled us to reach this occasion."[10]

9. This broadcast can be heard at http://www.youtube.com/watch?v=Vy_LlKE9OMQ.

10. "Rising from the Ashes . . .," *Your People, My People*, Apr. 20, 2102, http://www.yourpeoplemypeople.org/2012/04/rising-from-ashes.html.

About the Author

 RABBI REUVEN TRAVIS SPENT fifteen years as an advertising and marketing executive. He developed strategic business and marketing plans for a variety of consumer packaged-goods and financial-services companies. He was responsible for implementation of these plans, including managing multimillion-dollar budgets.

Fifteen years ago, Rabbi Travis started his career as an educator. He is currently on the faculty of Atlanta's only Modern Orthodox high school, where he teaches American History, AP U.S. Government, Jewish History, and Chumash.

Rabbi Travis earned his bachelor's degree from Dartmouth College, where he graduated Phi Beta Kappa with a double major in French literature and political science. He holds a Master of Arts in Jewish Studies from Spertus College and a Master of Arts in Teaching from Mercer University. He received his rabbinic ordination from Rabbi Michael J. Broyde, dean of Atlanta Torah MiTzion Kollel, after spending four years studying with Rabbi Broyde and the members of the kollel.

In 2013, Rabbi Travis was named the Distinguished High School Educator of the Year by the Georgia Commission on the Holocaust for his instruction on civil rights in his American History courses. That same year, he was also named as a Natalia Twersky Award finalist by the Jewish Women's Archive.

Bibliography

Andersen, Frances I. *Job*. Tyndale Old Testament Commentaries Series. Downers Grove, IL: InterVarsity Press, 1976.

Balentine, Samuel E. *Job*. Macon, GA: Smyth & Helwys, 2006.

Barkley, Russell A., and Christine M. Benton. *Your Defiant Child: Eight Steps to Better Behavior*. New York: Guilford Press, 1998.

Besdin, Abraham R. "The Holocaust and the State of Israel: Are They Related?" In *Theological and Halakhic Reflections on the Holocaust*, edited by Bernhard H. Rosenberg and Fred Heuman, 137–43. Hoboken, NJ: Ktav, 1972.

Blumenthal, David R. *Facing the Abusing God: A Theology of Protest*. Louisville, KY: Westminster John Knox, 1993.

Brown, Robert. Introduction to *The Trial of God (as it was held on February 25, 1649, in Shamgorod)*, by Elie Wiesel, vii–xix. Translated by Marion Wiesel. New York: Schocken Books, 1979.

Buber, Martin. *At the Turning*. New York: Farrar, Straus & Young, 1952.

Carson, Donald A. *How Long, O Lord? Reflections on Suffering and Evil*. Grand Rapids, MI: Baker, 1990.

Cox, Claude E. "Iob." In *A New English Translation of the Septuagint*, edited by Albert Pietersma and Benjamin G. Wright, 667–96. Oxford: Oxford University Press, 2007. Online: ccat.sas.upenn.edu/nets/edition/28-iob-nets.pdf.

Crenshaw, James L. "Job." In *The Oxford Bible Commentary*, edited by John Barton and John Muddiman, 354. Oxford: Oxford University Press, 2001.

———. *Old Testament Wisdom: An Introduction*. London: SCM, 1982.

Curtis, John Briggs. "On Job's Response to Yahweh." *JBL* 98 (1979) 497–511.

Eisen, Robert. *The Book of Job in Medieval Jewish Philosophy*. New York: Oxford University Press, 2004.

Goldwurn, Hersh, and Nosson Scherman, eds. *Talmud Bavli, Schottenstein Edition*. ArtScroll Series. 6 vols. Brooklyn: Mesorah, 1997.

Goodman, Lenn E. *The Book of Theodicy: Translation and Commentary on the Book of Job by Saadiah Ben Joseph Al- Fayyu*[set macron over u]*mi*[set macron over i]*; Translated from the Arabic with a Philological Commentary*. New Haven: Yale University Press, 1988.

Gordis, Robert. *The Book of Job: Commentary, New Translation and Special Studies*. New York: Jewish Theological Seminary of America, 1978.

Grunblatt, J. "The Great Estrangement: The Rabbi and the Student." *Tradition* 8, no. 2 (1966) 66–73.

Bibliography

Guttmann, Joseph. *The Philosophy of Judaism: The History of Jewish Philosophy from Biblical Times to Franz Rosenzweig.* Translated by David W. Silverman. 1933. Reprint, Northvale, NJ: J. Aronson, 1988.

Habel, Norman. *The Book of Job.* Old Testament Library. London: SCM, 1983.

Helfgot, Nathaniel. "Unlocking the Riddle of Abraham the Iconoclast: A Study in the Intertextuality of Peshat and Derash." *Tradition* 43, no. 3 (2010) 9–16.

Hicks, Joshua Mark. "Faithful Lament: Job's Response to Suffering." Paper given at the Lipscomb University Sermon Seminar, Harding University Graduate School of Religion, Memphis, TN, May 10–12, 1999. Online: http://johnmarkhicks.wordpress.com/general-articleslectures/.

Janzen, J. Gerald. *Job.* Interpretation. Atlanta: John Knox Press, 1985.

"Job." *Jewish Encyclopedia.* Online: http://www.jewishencyclopedia.com/articles/8692-job.

Josephus. *The Jewish War.* Translated by G. A. Williamson. New York: Dorset Press, 1981.

Kaplan, L. J. "Maimonides, Dale Patrick, and Job xli 6." *Vetus Testamentum* 28 (1978) 356–57.

Krüger, Thomas. "Did Job Repent?" In *Das Buch Hiob und seine Interpretationen: Beiträge zum Hiob-Symposium auf dem Monte Verità vom 14.–19. August 2005*, edited by T. Krüger et al., 217–29. Abhandlungen zur Theologie des Alten und Neuen Testaments 88. Zurich: Theologischer Verlag, 2007.

Lawson, Steven J. *When All Hell Breaks Loose.* Colorado Springs: NavPress, 1994.

Leibowitz, Nehama. *Studies in Bereishit (Genesis).* Translated by Aryeh Newman. 1972. Reprint, Jerusalem: Alpha Press, 1981.

Lookstein, Haskel. "Parshat Ki Tavoh, September 16, 2000." *OU Torah Insights Project.* Pearl and Harold M. Jacobs Shabbat Learning Center. Online: http://www.ou.org/torah/ti/5760/kitavo60.htm.

Lustiger, Arnold. *Before Hashem You Shall Be Purified: Rabbi Joseph B. Soloveitchik on the Days of Awe.* Edison, NJ: Ohr, 1998.

Maimonides, Moses. *The Guide for the Perplexed.* Translated by Shlomo Pines. Chicago: University of Chicago Press, 1963.

McCabe, Robert V. "Elihu's Contribution to the Thought of the Book of Job." *Detroit Baptist Seminary Journal* 2 (1997) 47–80.

McKenzie, R. A. F., and Roland E. Murphy. "Job." In *The New Jerome Biblical Commentary*, edited by Raymond E. Brown, Joseph A. Fitzmyer, and Roland E. Murphy, 488. London: Geoffrey Chapman, 1989.

Michel, W. L. "Did Job or God Repent? Job 42:5–6: Ellipses and Janus Parallelism in Job's Final Response to an Abusive God and the Message of the Book of Job." Unpublished paper, 2002.

Morrow, William. "Consolation, Rejection, and Repentance in Job 42:6." *Journal of Biblical Literature* 105 (1986) 211–25.

Muffs, Yochanan. *Love and Joy: Law, Language, and Religion in Ancient Israel.* New York: Jewish Theological Seminary of America, 1992.

Nachmanides, Moses. *Commentary on the Torah.* Translated by Charles B. Chavel. 5 vols. New York: Shilo, 1974.

Newsom, Carol A. *The Book of Job: A Contest of Moral Imaginations.* Oxford: Oxford University Press, 2003.

———. "Job." In vol. 4 of *The New Interpreter's Bible*, by Robert Doran et al., 628–29. Nashville: Abingdon, 1996.

Patrick, Dale. "The Translation of Job xlii 6." *Vetus Testamentum* 26, no. 3 (1976) 369–71.

PBS. "Teaching Guide, Activity Two: Bearing Witness." *Elie Wiesel: First Person Singular.* Online: http://www.pbs.org/eliewiesel/teaching/activity2.html.

Ravitzky, Aviezer. *Messianism, Zionism and Jewish Religious Radicalism.* Chicago: University of Chicago Press, 1996.

Reeves, Phil. "Holocaust Victims Were Punished for Sins of Their Past Lives, Claims Eminent Rabbi." *The Independent*, Aug. 7, 2000. Online: http://www.independent. co.uk/news/world/middle-east/holocaust-victims-were-punished-for-sins-of-their-past-lives-claims-eminent-rabbi-711566.html.

Rosenberg, Bernhard H., and Fred Heuman, eds. *Theological and Halakhic Reflections on the Holocaust.* Hoboken, NJ: Ktav, 1992.

Sachar, Howard M. *A History of Israel from the Rise of Zionism to Our Time.* New York: Alfred A. Knopf, 1976.

Safire, William. *The First Dissident: The Book of Job in Today's Politics.* New York: Random House, 1992.

Schneerson, Menahem Mendel. *Sefer ha-sihot, 5751.* Brooklyn, NY: Kehot Publication Society, 1993.

Schreiner, Susan E. *Where Shall Wisdom Be Found? Calvin's Exegesis of Medieval and Modern Perspectives.* Chicago: University of Chicago Press, 1994.

Senor, Dan, and Saul Singer. *Start-Up Nation: The Story of Israel's Economic Miracle.* New York: Twelve, 2009.

Shapira, K. K. *Sacred Fire: Torah from the Years of Fury, 1939–1942.* Translated by J. Hershey Worch. Northvale, NJ: J. Aronson, 2002.

Shoah Resource Center. "Jewish Philosophical and Theological Responses to the Holocaust." International School for Holocaust Studies. Online: http://www1. yadvashem.org/odot_pdf/microsoft%20word%20-%206385.pdf.

Skinner, Burrhus F. *Science and Human Behavior.* New York: Free Press, 1953.

Soloveitchik, Joseph B. *Abraham's Journey: Reflections on the Life of the Founding Patriarch.* Jersey City, NJ: Ktav, 2008.

———. *Days of Deliverance: Essays on Purim and Hanukkah.* Jersey City, NJ: Ktav, 2007.

———. *Halakhic Man.* Edited by D. Shatz, J. B. Wolowelsky, and R. Ziegler. Philadelphia: Jewish Publication Society of America, 1983.

———. "Kol Dodi Dofek: It Is the Voice of My Beloved That Knocketh." In *Theological and Halakhic Reflections on the Holocaust*, edited by B. H. Rosenberg and F. Heuman, 51–117. Hoboken, NJ: Ktav, 1972.

———. *Out of the Whirlwind: Essays on Mourning, Suffering and the Human Condition.* Jersey City, NJ: Ktav, 2003.

Stedman, Ray C. *What's This World Coming To? An Expository Study of Matthew 24–26, the Olivet Discourse.* Palo Alto, CA: Discovery Publications, 1970.

Ticciati, Susannah. *Job and the Disruption of Identity: Reading Beyond Barth.* London: T&T Clark, 2005.

Voorst, Bruce van. "Dust and Ashes." *Christian Century* 125, no. 17 (2008) 28–32.

Walters, L. "Reflections on Suffering from the Book of Job." *Bibliotheca Sacra* 154 (1997) 436–51.

Weber, Robertus, ed. *Idcirco ipse me reprehendo et ago paenitentiam in favilla et cinere: Biblia Sacra Iuxta Vulgatam Versionem.* 2 vols. 2nd ed. Stuttgart: Wurttembergische Bibelanstalt, 1975.

Bibliography

Wiesel, Elie. Interview by R. Gardner and D. Grossbach. *First Person Singular*. PBS, October 24, 2002.

———. *Messengers of God: Biblical Portraits and Legends*. Translated by Marion Wiesel. New York: Random House, 1976.

———. *Night*. Translated by Stella Rodway. New York: Bantam, 1982.

———. Nobel lecture. December 11, 1986. Online: http://nobelprize.org/nobel_prizes/peace/laureates/1986/wiesel-lecture.html.

———. *The Trial of God (as it was held on February 25, 1649, in Shamgorod)*. Translated by Marion Wiesel. New York: Schocken Books, 1979.

Wilson, Leslie S. *The Book of Job: Judaism in the 2nd Century BCE: An Intertextual Reading*. Lanham, MD: University Press of America, 2006.

Wolde, Ellen J. van. "Job 42,1–6: The Reversal of Job." In *The Book of Job*, edited by W. A. M. Beuken, 223–50. Leuven: Leuven University Press/Uitgeverij Peeters, 1994.

Wolpe, David. "For Argument's Sake." *Jewish Week*, Oct. 23, 2009, p. 7.

Wolters, Al. "'A Child of Dust and Ashes' (Job 42, 6b)." *Zeitschrift für die alttestamentliche Wissenschaft* 102 (1990) 116–19.

Wright, Jacob. "A Nation Conceived in Defeat." *Azure* 43 (2010) 83–101.

Zeitlin, Solomon. *The Rise and Fall of the Judean State*. Philadelphia: Jewish Publication Society, 1962.